PETERHEAD PORRIDGE

PETERHEAD PORRIDGE

TALES FROM THE FUNNY SIDE OF
SCOTLAND'S MOST NOTORIOUS PRISON

JAMES CROSBIE

BLACK & WHITE PUBLISHING

First published 2007
by Black & White Publishing Ltd
99 Giles Street, Edinburgh EH6 6BZ

ISBN 13: 978 1 84502 152 8
ISBN 10: 1 84502 152 5

A CIP catalogue record for this book is available
from the British Library.

Typeset by GreenGate Publishing Services, Tonbridge, Kent
Printed and bound by Nørhaven Paperback A/S

For all the characters – screws and cons alike
– who made life in the old Peterhead Prison
that little bit more bearable

CONTENTS

INTRODUCTION

There is no question that of all the prisons I have been in, Peterhead was certainly the most colourful and, if I dare say so, interesting. I'm sorry now that I didn't keep a more accurate record of the madcap people and goings on in there. I say madcap because that's exactly what they were. I mean, where else but in a prison could you hope to meet people with exotic nicknames like **Rent A Rope**, **Raving Rampton Rab**, **Batman**, **Bald Eagle**, **The Saughton Harrier** and **Sodjer Thompson**? All ably supported by guys like **Flame On**, **Davie Doughnut**, **The Mad Major**, **Rab The Cat** and **Stinky Steve** and not forgetting **Gentle Johnny**, **Big Nellie**, and even **The Godfather** himself, to name just a few of the men who did hard time in Peterhead.

And the screws had their fair share too – **Fairy Queen**, **Banana Back**, **Bible John**, **Cement Heid** and **Hank The Yank**, all of whom worked alongside **Gibbering Gibby**, **Red Alert**, **Deputy Dawg**, **Hess**, **Jelly Buttocks** and **The Gimp**. With handles like that, along with many other exotically named screws, there have to be some fascinating tales to tell. And when you find out that the prisoners christened the governor **Slasher Gallagher** you just know there has to be a story behind his name.

Believe me, this is a prison story with a difference. I have used nicknames as the main theme of this book but I have also included some outlandish escapades that were carried out by both cons and screws alike. Needless to say, there are good reasons behind all these nicknames, some obvious some not so obvious, but every name and every story is guaranteed to make you laugh. Furthermore, everything in this book actually happened – and lots more besides!

1

THE ROAD TO PETERHEAD

I suppose it is only fair to say that my personal road to Peterhead actually began the day I entered the Hillington branch of the Clydesdale Bank in Glasgow, in April 1974, and walked out ten minutes later carrying a bag containing around £67,000 in hard cash. Needless to say, I had withdrawn this cash without the benefit of having an account, thus avoiding the bothersome business of filling in a withdrawal slip. In simple English, I had robbed the bank.

There had been no need for me to rob this bank – or any of the others that followed, for that matter. You see, in 1974, I was doing very well for myself, having built up a furniture importing and retail business in my hometown district of Springburn, Glasgow. Happily married with a wife and young son, I was enjoying life in a pleasant suburb of the city. I led an active social life, enjoying nights out with my wife, playing golf and had recently qualified as a private pilot. In fact, everything was going well for me but greed, circumstance and opportunity intervened and, instead of concentrating on my business, I found myself robbing banks.

But this story is not about my bank-robbing proclivities – I only mention them here to inform the reader of the reason I took the high road to Peterhead. This story is about life and the many oddball characters I met in the madness of that high-security prison.

However, the real road to Peterhead, and by this I mean the metalled road, not a metaphorical road that is paved by a wayward lifestyle, started for me at the gates of Edinburgh's Saughton Prison.

There were about eight of us on the fortnightly draft to the penal outpost of Peterhead and the journey began in an almost carnival atmosphere, with cons cheerfully passing round precious tobacco and sharing treasured sweets as they cracked jokes and made outrageous observations about the passing world beyond the confines of their bus. But the carefree convict carry-on and false bravado did not last for many miles. Handcuffed two by two, we travelled with darkened barred windows, doors securely chained and a sawdust-filled bucket for a toilet. We were guarded by six surly, uncommunicative screws who soon destroyed the fleeting illusion of freedom – it wasn't a bus we were on, it was a travelling jailhouse.

Gradually we withdrew into a quiet, introspective silence as the bus drove us steadily northwards, pausing first at Perth Prison and then advancing to Aberdeen, like pawns on a chessboard, until finally it was check-in and checkmate at Peterhead.

Well, I was back and I did not like it at all. My previous sentence at PH had been just eighteen months and that had seemed long and hard at the time. But now . . . twenty years? TWENTY YEARS! Wow!!! How was I going to do it? I must admit felt pretty numb as I endured the reception process. It was very depressing, sitting on a concrete stool in a cold cell of the punishment block, waiting for my name to be called out and then hearing the tramp, tramp, tramp of approaching feet and the rattle of keys as a screw unlocked the door and led me through to the reception desk.

'Crosbie?' The reception screw looked up from his papers and spoke down at me as I stood in front of his high, schoolmaster's desk.

'Yes.' I had long since learned to be economical with answers in jail.

The screw studied me for a moment or two, a slight questioning look on his face. 'Crosbie, James,' he gave me my full name in reverse and continued his query. 'Twenty years?' He sounded sceptical, as if he had made a mistake.

'That's right,' I confirmed.

'You're Crosbie!' He looked me up and down and there was no doubting the surprise in his voice. By now, I was beginning to think that maybe there had been some mistake.

'Yes, that's me,' I confirmed.

'Huh!' His snort was very definitely disparaging and he had a distinctly disappointed look as he began to process me.

I didn't realise it then but I later found out that my appearance had been most disappointing to him. He had obviously been aware that I was arriving on the draft bus and had conjured up an image of some huge, thick-necked, brawny, bald-headed, TV stereotype of a bank-robber who was well worth slapping with a twenty-year sentence. But it was only me and there I stood in front of him – five foot eight inches and a full ten and a half stone and about as threatening as a high street handbag snatcher. He was definitely not impressed. And it appeared that the resident gangsters had also seriously misjudged me, obviously equating the size of the man to the size of the jobs he had pulled – a fact that became clear when I was handed a cardboard box containing my prison-issue clothing. In anticipation of my arrival, the gangsters of PH had had my uniform and shirts specially made up for me in the prison's tailors' shop.

The only problem was the clothes would have fitted John Wayne. The shirtsleeves dangled past my wrists like two flapping sheets and the jacket would have looked loose on Mike Tyson.

I was very definitely a disappointment to the welcoming committee of known Glasgow 'faces'. I even caught one of them looking at me in shock. He screwed up his face in consternation and mouthed to his mate in tones of amazement, 'Is that him?' Yes, I'm afraid it is, pal, I thought to myself as I was escorted up to my security cell on the third floor of A Hall.

The day after my arrival, as the final part of the reception procedure, I was marched in front of the current governor, a kindly old soul (for up there anyway) called Angus, and officially 'welcomed' to Peterhead Penitentiary. You often hear of people being described as a 'fatherly figure' – not so often prison governors, though – but that was exactly what old Angus was. He never ranted and raved, was never vindictive, did his daily rounds of the workshops with a tolerant smile on his face and accepted the misbehaviour of his charges with a reproachful look and sad shake of his head as he imposed his inevitable penalties on them. But, like all prison governors, Angus was merely a figurehead. The real power in any prison in those days was with the chief officer. It still is but they have different titles nowadays and wear suits instead of uniforms. But, a rose by any other name . . .

So it was Chief Officer **Gibbering Gibby** who took it upon himself to put me in my place. 'You! You, Crosbie! You're the one that robbed all those banks. Aye, well there will be no bank robbing here.' (He wasn't called Gibbering Gibby for nothing, you see.) 'Ye'll behave yourself in this

4

place – I'll see tae that. Tailors' shop for you, m'laddie. Security party – that's where you're going. And, mind ye, I'll be keeping my eye on you!' And that was that. My reception was complete. I was in the jail and in my place – all sorted out in a matter of minutes.

Routine is the staff of life in prison and, strangely enough, it is this very routine, whether they realise it or not, that enables most prisoners to handle their time inside. It is hard to explain but the fact is that the more time you are doing the less important time seems to be. I've known guys doing eighteen months who have every day counted out. They can tell you how many dinners they have to come, how many Sundays they have left to go or how their lib (liberation) date falls on a Saturday or Sunday so they 'steal' a day or two by getting out on the Friday before. Some of them could even tell you, to the hour, how long they have to go. They have every single day ticked off and counted, like the drip, drip, drip of the Chinese water torture. Now that's doing time!

It is a paradox that the longer you are serving the less likely you are to count out the time. You see, long-termers put the future out of their minds. Everything is so far away that there is no point in making plans or thinking about it. Of course birthdays and anniversaries come round and cards are sent. Christmases come and Christmases go, friends and family marry, nephews and nieces are born, people die and life goes on outside. But your world stops at the gate and you have got to learn to live in jail.

The world of prison has only two seasons and few memorable dates. The year is divided into summer and winter, or to put it another way – light nights and dark nights. The light nights start in April when the clock springs forward and the dark nights kick in when the clock falls back again in October. Two other important dates are 21 July, the longest day of the year, and 22 December, the shortest day of the year. Christmas Day is of course always memorable as the season of goodwill, with extra food and a monetary gift from the common good fund and, if you are lucky, there might even be a show of some sort. Then of course there is New Year's Day – the Big Day! It's definitely the day most cons really think about their sentences. The old year has ended and a new one has begun and there is a generally happier atmosphere as men congratulate each other on being a year closer to their lib date. The lucky cons can say start talking about release that year and the second luckiest cons start saying things like, 'Cracked it. I'm out next year!' But, funnily enough, because they can now start talking realistically about getting out, their time starts to drag, as if they are now in the same position as short-termers themselves. But the thing is, other than the days or dates I have mentioned, every day in prison is strictly routine, with the result that they all meld into one and, before you know it, time has slipped away.

The secret to doing time, as I have already said, is that you have to learn to live in jail. Keep your head *inside* the prison and let routine anaesthetise you to time. Of course you will always have your memories but, when you think about the future, it will seem like a distant dream that's too unreal to have any effect.

Because my previous sentences had been fairly short, this was something I had yet to learn. And, besides, irrespective of the aforementioned philosophy, it takes most cons just over a year before the anaesthetic starts to kick in. When a con begins a sentence, any sentence, he will always make day-to-day comparisons with what he would be doing outside if he wasn't in the jail. His mind will revolve round memories like the weekend visit to the pub, the regular night out at the dogs, nights out with the wife or girlfriend and time spent with the kids. All the pleasurable activities that you could be doing instead of lying in a prison cell invade your mind and torment the hell out of you. And I bet many a hard-case convict has shed more than one regretful tear or two in the seclusion of a suddenly lonelier cell. The nostalgia can be overwhelming during that first year or so before the intense sense of loss gradually fades and you begin really living in the jail – I can testify to that. The average reader may not be able to relate to all that stuff but I bet any con or ex-con reading this will be nodding his head right now.

Well, explanations done, I can now start telling you about life in Peterhead. But I don't intend boring you with the oft-repeated litany of violence and hard times. I intend to show, mostly, the other side of life inside. I'll try to give you a picture of the many offbeat, nicknamed characters – screws and cons alike – who populated Peterhead and relate some of the stories that are handed down now as part of Scottish prison folklore.

2

A CONGLOMERATION OF CONVICTS

I've always liked words and phrases and I especially like collective nouns. My favourite word is 'serendipity' (look it up yourself!) although 'axiomatic' runs a close second. And my favourite collective noun is 'a murder of crows'. I think that particular phrase conjures up the perfect image of a gang of sinister, black-suited, beady-eyed killers waiting to swoop on their victim. But do you know something? I haven't ever heard of a good collective noun for convicts so I made one up – a conglomeration of convicts. I think that description is apt because that's exactly what they are – a mixed bunch of humanity struggling to survive in the hostile environment of prison. In this microcosm of society, there are the leaders and the led, the weak and the strong, the extrovert and the introvert and, even in Peterhead, the guys and the dolls. The only group of society missing from the population of Peterhead was intellectuals – probably because anyone with more than half a brain knew how to avoid the place.

With such a diverse conglomeration of humanity, it is no wonder there are stories to tell. But where to begin? Nicknames seem as good a place to start as anything to me because most sobriquets are earned and therein usually lies a tale. This is especially so in the criminal world, which abounds in colourful nicknames.

As the author of this work, it is only fair that I introduce myself by my own nickname which is **Bing**. And how did I earn it? Well, the older generation will immediately relate it to Bing Crosby (note the spelling), the well-known crooner and star of many films. The real Bing actually died during a round of golf in the year of 1977. As a matter of fact I was in Peterhead when his sad demise was announced on the radio – no TV sets in those days!

'Bing's dead!' I heard someone yelling out of their cell window, passing on the news.

Then I had to smile as a very unsympathetic voice replied, 'No wonder – he's always running round that exercise yard like a fucking madman!'

It always surprised me how aptly nicknames fitted individuals in Peterhead and this went for both screws and cons alike. I've already mentioned Gibbering Gibby, surely self-explanatory. And you don't need much of an imagination to picture the screw, **Jelly Buttocks**, waddling along the landing, his fat face red with exertion and his neck squeezed tight in his collar. His claim to fame was that he stuck Jimmy Boyle's head in a bucket of water and tried to drown him down the punishment block – or the **Dardanelles** (cells), as we called them. Then there was **Cement Heid** (Head), the product of an inbred fishing village community. He had earned his name on two separate counts: firstly, because he originally appeared in Peterhead making regular deliveries as the driver of a cement lorry.

After making deliveries for some weeks, Cement Heid realised that the uniformed prison officers he saw there did not appear to do very much in the way of actual physical exertion. Eventually he approached one of the screws. 'Fit like, min?' he said, using the Doric. He was actually asking, 'How are you, man?'

Upon receiving a satisfactory reply to this initial overture, Cement Heid now ventured the question that had obviously been puzzling him for some time. 'What is it you do? What's your job?'

'I'm a prison officer.' The population of the Blue Toon, as Peterhead is known locally, has never been well known for their conversational abilities.

'Aye, min, Ah ken 'at bit fit d'ye dee?' (This translates as 'Yes, man, I know that but what do you do?' For the sake of clarity, from now on, I'll stick mostly to proper English just throwing in the odd piece of local patois for flavour.)

'I stand here on guard.'

'You mean you don't actually do any work?' Cement Heid was becoming interested.

'This is my work,' the screw retorted. 'I just stand here and watch these prisoners.'

'And how many pennies a week dae ye get for that, min?' Cement Heid asked.

As the screw imparted the information, obviously naming a sum far in excess of his pecuniary expectations, Cement Heid's mouth fell open. 'What!' he gasped and even the cons recognised the excitement in his response. 'You get all that money just for standing watching them?'

The screw confirmed his salary then looked on in surprise as Cement Heid leapt into the cab of his lorry and roared off in a cloud of exhaust fumes. Two minutes later, the office staff were surprised to see a huge cement lorry pulling up outside the admin building and observed an excited Cement Heid bounding into their office.

'I want to join up,' Cement Heid announced. 'I want to become a prison officer.' And join up he did. Two weeks later, the ex-cement lorry driver was pounding the landings in A Hall, resplendent in his black uniform and shiny skip cap.

The second reason Cement Heid acquired his sobriquet was blindingly obvious – the idiot was as thick as two short planks. One of his more memorable blunders was when he approached a fellow officer and reported that he had got rid of a certain prisoner's pigeons. Now, pigeons were a big thing with some of the men in PH and, with so little else to do, they often became an obsession. Men would spend hours letting them fly from their cell windows and catering for their every need. Some of the men had even nurtured their pigeons from eggs laid in their cupboards by birds they already owned. The authorities turned a blind eye to the practice of keeping pigeons – after all, it was a harmless pastime and it did keep the men out of mischief. But somehow or other one of the men had fallen foul of Cement Heid, leaving himself open to attack, and the screw's revenge was swift and brutal.

'Aye, that's that', Cement Heid announced one day to his shift partner, the **Fairy Queen**. 'I soon got rid of that Jackson's pigeons.'

'Aye, min?' said Fairy Queen, nodding his approval. He was so named because of his definitely effeminate tendencies. He also had the habit of belting his uniform jacket up so tight that the hem stuck out from his hips like a ballerina's tutu. Curious, he added, 'An' how did you do that?'

'I put them out the window. They've flew away.'

'Och, don't be daft, min,' Fairy Queen retorted. 'That's no good. They're bloody homing pigeons. They'll be back the noo, ye ken.'

However, not wanting his colleague to be cheated out of his revenge, he unselfishly offered to help out. 'Come on,' he said, 'I'll show you how to get rid of them.'

And, with that, they both marched back to the prisoner's cell. The pigeons, as Fairy Queen had rightly predicted, had already returned and were happily cooing away on their perches on the window ledge.

Quite calmly Fairy Queen took one of the pigeons down and callously wrung its neck. 'There, that's the way to get rid of them, min,' he informed his appreciative audience. 'Just wring their bloody necks. They'll dae no more flying then'.

Nodding with enthusiastic agreement, Cement Heid followed Fairy Queen's example and a few quick twists of his wrists promptly despatched the rest of the innocent birds off to that great pigeon coop in the sky. Both officers were seen leaving the cell looking pleased with themselves and the four dead pigeons on the prisoner's table were clear evidence of their foul deed.

Talk about a furore! The con went ballistic and even some of the screws temporarily shelved their usual solidarity to voice objections at their colleagues' barbaric behaviour. However – and you had to give him credit for this – although the con knew who was responsible for killing his pigeons, he remained sensible enough to keep his hands to himself as he ranted and raved at the assassin. He did, however, decide to take what we all thought was the sensible course, hoping that Cement Heid would at least suffer some penalty for his crime. A letter reporting the incident was despatched to the Royal Society for the Protection of Birds and we all sat back waiting for retribution to descend on the ignorant, pigeon-killing Cement Heid.

I forget the precise wording of the letter the con received in reply to his outraged complaint but it went along the lines of:

The Society regrets the incident regarding the killing of your pigeons. However, we can only act if the behaviour of the individual concerned led to the birds suffering cruelty or undue pain and suffering. Furthermore, as pigeons are regarded as vermin, such a method of despatch is considered to be humane and, in this case, we can take no action against the individual concerned.

Yours sincerely, etc. etc.

End of story.

Jesus! The pigeons were the man's pets – his friends and companions during the lonely hours in his cell. They even served to give some meaning to his life in jail. Vermin! We were all disgusted and Cement Heid continued to stand guard on the landing with a self-satisfied smirk on his face. If it wasn't for the fact that he had already been given a very appropriate nickname, he would undoubtedly have been dubbed 'Pigeon Killer' from then on. But, then again, the fact that he *had* killed the pigeons only endorsed his entitlement to be forever known as Cement Heid.

Yes, nicknames always seem to fit the individuals they are given to, especially those earned by some physical deformity. Names like **Limpy**, **Big Ears**, **Banana Back**, **Specs**, **Beaky**, **Deefy** (he was deaf), **One Lamp** (he only had one eye) and **The Gimp**, to mention just a few, immediately present an image so clear that you would probably recognise the person so called even if you had never seen them before. Other nicknames could be earned through deeds or, more often, misdeeds. **Gas Meter John**, **The Mad Biker**, **Karate Joe**, **Flame On**, **Tam The Tapper** (he was always borrowing things), **Batman** and **Slasher** are all amazingly appropriate. I could write them out by the dozen but I'll just let you come across them as I relate a few of the incidents in Peterhead carried out by Scotland's toughest!

Funnily enough, the coining of nicknames seems to be dying out nowadays. It's a shame because they contributed a lot of the colour and variety of life in jail. It seems that, except for the odd irrepressible individuals, we have all descended into the same prison greyness of nameless mediocrity.

3

HADGEY'S HAMMER HORROR

Every prison has its daily routine. The very mention of the word conjures up visions of a dull, boring existence, particularly when it's applied to prison. Every day begins the same: 7 a.m. unlock and, to this very day at the time of writing in 2007, slop out; breakfast at 7.30; then, at 8.00, it's outside into the yard, rain, hail or snow, to line up in your work parties, like POWs being counted before being marched off to the workshops. In my case, it was the tailors' workshop. Once the cons were in their workplaces anything could and, from time to time, did happen.

The tailors' workshop was located in an old, red granite, villa-style building in the outer yard of the jail along with the other workshops, like the joiners' shop, the mat shop and that old prison favourite, the concrete party.

There was also non-stop work on the **Burma Road** – a building project named after that infamous highway the Japanese forced prisoners of war to build through the torturous jungle of Burma during the Second World War. This Burma Road project had been going on for years within the walls of Peterhead and was simply a bunch of press-ganged cons repeatedly digging up and flattening out the earthen road-cum-track that led to the prison workshops. It wouldn't surprise me if work on the Burma Road was still going on to this very day.

On my first working day in Peterhead, I lined up with the other security men to be marched through the inner gate and down the Burma Road to the tailors' shop – aye, the tailors' shop. Christ, don't tell me I'm getting nostalgic about the place? Nah! Surely it couldn't be that? But writing about it certainly brings back memories. And what memories too! I was witness to everything in that workshop – near-fatal stabbings, practical jokes, crazy killers telling crazier tales and cons playing interminable prison pastime games.

It would be impossible to report on all of the players who starred in the continuous workshop soap opera that was PH security party. I dare say there were never so many murderers, armed robbers and other viciously violent criminals working together in the same place at the same time. The very fact that each individual had ended up in Peterhead in itself meant that every one of them had a unique, often bizarre, story to tell. And just to give you a taste of the really bizarre, I'll tell you about **Hadgey**.

To say Hadgey was a lowbrow would simply be stating a literal fact. With a forehead that sloped downward at almost forty-five degrees, ending up in a thick thatch of eyebrow fur that shadowed the deep hollows of his sunken eyes, Hadgey could easily have been mistaken for a walking, talking Piltdown man. Huge in the shoulder and strong as an ox, this modern day Neanderthal worked on the sewing machine next to mine – elbow to elbow, you might say – and, naturally, we talked about our cases. It didn't matter that all the details of a con's case had been widely reported in the press, other cons still thirsted for the *inside* story – even although every word that had appeared in print had been minutely pored over and discussed in detail. Being a notorious bank robber, I was approached on a regular basis as convicts came and went and, of course, I was privy to many an inside tale myself. Hadgey's story is just one of the many revelations that would make even a Hammer House of Horror scriptwriter recoil.

How do you start a conversation with a madman? Well, there is a trick to it and the trick is you've got to pretend both to him and yourself that he's not mad. You've got to learn to treat these nutcases with kid gloves and talk to them in a perfectly normal conversational manner. You must listen to them as if their story is simply part and parcel of normal daily life.

It was one of those days when we had become tired of playing games like hangman, battleships and cruisers, noughts and crosses and quiz games and our conversation turned to Hadgey's crime. Usually these sorts of conversations begin with the simple question, 'How long are you doing, then?' But this is merely a ploy to pave the way for the next question which is, 'What did you get that for?' It doesn't really matter that, nine times out of ten, you already know the answers to these questions – it's just a polite opening gambit to get the guy to tell his tale and many's the tale I heard too. But I have to admit Hadgey's story takes the top prize. Well . . . maybe not when I think about it. There was another guy who butchered most of his family and as the police were dragging him out of the house he was shouting, 'Aye and I done the dog as well!' However, for now, I will tell you Hadgey's tale.

'How long are you doing?' I said, casually offering the accepted opening gambit to Hadgey one day. The fact that I did already know the answer was neither here nor there – I was simply employing the conventional method of opening up the conversation. However, it is essential to inject a note of surprise when your question is answered – especially when the answer is 'Life.'

'Life!' It is important to adopt a tone that suggests some wrong may have been done by the courts in terms of the severity of the sentence.

'What did you get that for?' And the scene is set for another riveting revelation.

'Strangled a fucking dwarf.' It wasn't exactly monosyllabic but, without any elaboration of any kind, it sounded rather stark to say the least. But you mustn't recoil or look in any way shocked at this bald statement of fact. It is, after all, just a *normal* conversation – for Peterhead, that is.

'Oh, aye. And what did you do that for, Hadgey?' The case had been all over the papers but you have to follow protocol in these delicate matters.

'Caught the wee bastard shagging ma burd.'

'Oh, did you? So . . . well . . . what happened then?' Meantime we are stitching and sewing away at our task of producing prison clothing.

'Ah telt ye! Ah caught him at it wi' her and strangled him.'

'He was dead?'

'Aye, he was deid all right. Ah telt ye. Ah strangled the wee bastard.'

'Aye, well, so that was him dead. Then what did you do?'

At this, Hadgey stopped work to explain how he coped with this unusual inconvenience. 'Well, he was deid so I decided I had to get rid of the body.'

I nodded encouragingly, showing keen interest.

'I decided to cut him up,' he told me.

'Aye, right enough,' I said, trying to keep things conversational. 'You would need to do that all right.'

Hadgey leant towards me and spoke earnestly, as if sharing a secret. 'But I knew, if I cut him up, he would bleed all over the place.'

'Yes.' I could only agree with this sentiment and sympathise with his predicament. 'So what did you do?'

'I got hold of a Black & Decker electric drill and bored a hole right on the top of his heid. Right through his skull I went. But see when I went to pour his blood doon the sink . . .?'

'Aye?' I admit I was a little puzzled at this but I tried to look serious as he continued his lurid tale.

'See when I tipped him over the sink and tried to empty the blood oot . . . you know something?'

'What?' I dared to ask.

'It never came oot. The blood just stayed there – stuck in his body.'

'Did it?' I didn't really have to feign surprise. Obviously the workings of the human body were a complete mystery to the intellectually challenged Hadgey. And, yet, when you think about it, he had no hesitation in applying himself to the dismemberment of a dwarf! The mind boggles.

'Naw,' he explained with a mystified shake of his head. 'Nothing. Not a drap.'

'So what did you do then?' I asked. This was better than *Tales from the Crypt*.

'I had an old hacksaw in the house so I got him on to the kitchen table and cut his heid off. Then I got his hands and arms off but the saw blade broke when I was cutting through his thigh.'

'Did it now?' I tut-tutted in disapproval at the failing quality of the British hacksaw blade.

'So that was me fucked.' Hadgey nodded regretfully at the memory.

'How?' I queried. 'You could always have got another blade.'

'Naw,' he tapped the side of his nose in a knowing way. 'I'm too wide for that. Right out of character that would have been. A dead give-away.'

'Aye, well, right enough.' Hadgey's logic was definitely giving me problems. 'So what *did* you do?'

'I got a big fire going in the grate and decided to burn it.'

'Aye?'

'I stuck the feet in first and they were burning away fine but there was a helluva smell and I had to stop.'

I looked at him and nodded sympathetically. 'So?'

'So I decided to phone my lawyer and ask him to come round to the house. I told him it was a big case.'

'Did he come?' I asked

'Aye, he came all right,' the bold Hadgey told me. 'But when he saw the heid on the table and a couple of hands lying on the sideboard he took a right flaky – ran oot the hoose and grassed me to the polis. And he was supposed to be *my* fucking lawyer!'

'The bastard!' I roundly condemned the treachery of the man. 'He got you jailed!'

'Ah, well,' Hadgey waxed philosophical. 'I would have been done anyway. You see, my burd had run away and told her pal about me strangling the fucking midget and the word was oot. When the polis came, I just admitted it and got a lifer.' He looked over at me and accepted my sympathetic mutterings as his due and, without a pause, continued speaking. 'Here, pass me over the quick-pick a minute, pal – I've ran on a few extra stitches here. And, by the way,' he remarked, after a few seconds of delicate snipping, 'do you know what my psychiatrist said to me?'

'No.' I shook my head and waited for his next revelation.

'He said,' Hadgey nodded slowly, knowingly, and repeated the words again. 'He said that I was one of the cleverest murderers he had ever met. And do you know why he said that?'

'No, I don't,' I told him. 'Why did he say that, Hadgey?'

'Because I tried to get rid of the body.'

And that was the tale of just one of the guys in the tailors' shop.

Anyway, as time passed, I settled into life in Peterhead, becoming part of the place and getting on with my sentence and fitting in quite well with my criminal contemporaries. But I was soon to discover that my convict mates were not the only madmen in the asylum. **Red Alert**, for example, was a screw who got his name from a sudden, ill-advised action he undertook one day in the tailors' shop.

New to the service, he had yet to make his mark and, up until the day of his official 'christening', he was known, for obvious reasons, as **Baby Face**. His introduction to guard duty in the tailors' shop, just a few short weeks after joining the service, was well out of order. He was thrown in at the deep end by fellow officers who resented the seniority status he enjoyed. This was because, although he was brand-new to the Prison Service, he carried forward seniority from his previous job in the local taxation office. Therefore, if he had the seniority, the bitchy old-time screws reasoned, he could shoulder the responsibilities such seniority warranted. So it was a baptism of fire in the tailors' shop for Baby Face.

To say he was a bundle of nerves would be an understatement. Primed by exaggerated reports from his fellow screws of the dangers from the unpredictable top-security prisoners, Baby Face stood nervously against the rear wall of the shop anxiously counting and recounting his charges. Resplendent in his shiny, new peaked cap, he braced himself against a radiator, careful not to catch anyone's eye and so avoid a confrontation with any of these dangerous prisoners.

Two men, Bill MacPherson, serving a twenty-five for armed bank robbery, and Tony Tunilla, doing a twelve for the same thing, sat directly in front of Baby Face in the back row of machines and recognised immediately that he was a total nervous wreck. It so happened that, outside but within sight of the window, a con was working away at the prison incinerator and was, at that very moment, digging a small pit. Billy Mac gave Tony T. a wink and nodded out the window towards the distant figure.

'How's the tunnel getting on?' he asked in a hoarse stage whisper.

Tony pretended to look surreptitiously out towards the incinerator where he could clearly see the con digging lustily with his spade. 'It's going well,' he answered in a low voice that just carried to Baby Face. 'He must have dug a good bit out by now.'

Baby Face nearly keeled over at the words as, leaning at an angle of almost forty-five degrees, he eavesdropped on the 'escape plot' unfolding before him.

'Has he got the rope and the hook organised yet?' Mac muttered.

'No problem. It's all been well stashed. We'll be ready to go any day now.'

Obviously not even stopping to consider what use a rope and hook would be in a tunnel, Baby Face launched himself into action and, in doing so, he earned himself the sobriquet that would henceforth follow him throughout the rest of his service life.

'Red alert! Red alert!'

Baby Face screamed the words at the top of his voice as he raced down the shop to expose the infamy. He burst into the office and yelled at Principal Officer Instructor

Robertson, 'Red alert, Mr Robertson, red alert! They're digging a tunnel and . . . and . . .' He stuttered to a halt as Robertson, otherwise known as **Bible John**, looked at him and slowly shook his head from side to side.

'And how do you know about this?' Bible John asked, totally unperturbed at the alarming news.

'I heard them,' Red Alert, his new name taking immediate effect, blurted out. 'Those two at the back, they were talking about it and, if you look out the window, you'll see they've got someone digging a tunnel!'

'Oh, a tunnel is it? Bible John dragged Red Alert back up to his station to confront the grinning Billy Mac and Tony T. 'You two stop messing about now,' he told them. 'And as for you, you idiot,' he cuffed the red-faced rookie on the back of his head in time with his words. 'Don't you be so stupid. Red alert?' He shook his head. 'You bloody idiot!'

And that's how you get a nickname.

As for Bible John . . . well, he acquired his nickname because he bore a striking resemblance to a witness's description and a police identikit photograph of a man wanted for the murder of three women in Glasgow. It was also known that the suspected killer, whose identity remains unknown to this day, was in the habit of quoting scripture to his victims. Apparently our own PO Robertson looked so similar to the description and identikit photo of the wanted man that someone, probably another screw, informed the police that Bible John was alive and well and working in Peterhead Penitentiary as a prison officer. This information, along with the fact that Robertson was an elder in a local church, led to the police interviewing him regarding his whereabouts at the time of the murders and from that moment on he was called nothing other than Bible John.

As a postscript to this, it has to be pointed out that the real Bible John was never captured and, believe me, I've seen the identikit photos and the resemblance between the two men is uncanny.

4

HANK THE YANK AND SHITTY BREEKS

For a prison work party, it has to be said that the tailors' shop in PH was never a dull place. As well as the usual subversive activities of sabotaging the machines, destroying material and setting elaborate incendiary devices, there were always games to be played and stories to be told. And even some of the screws got into the story-telling action. For instance, there was **Hank The Yank**.

Hank was a screw who had apparently spent some time in the USA. No one really knew if he had ever actually been to America but he continuously boasted of his life there in an obviously desperate attempt to impress the cons. The thing is we never ever got the stories at first hand from Hank. You see, it wasn't the done thing for an officer to converse with prisoners and give out information about his private life, past or present, so Hank developed a technique that allowed him to impart his information at second-hand.

He would stand against the radiator at the head of the stairs and engage his opposite number in conversation across the width of the workshop floor, loudly relating stories of his past life in Vegas. Hank made constant references to Frank, Dino, Sammy, Gina and other well known names, as if they were familiar boozing buddies of his, never quite fully identifying them, simply leaving it all to our imagination whom he was referring to. He regularly described wild nights out with the gang, describing how he beat Dino at golf and how he organised things in the Sands. The Flamingo Hotel, too, seemed flamboyant enough to receive many a mention in the course of this tales. According to Hank, he practically ran Vegas.

Eventually PO Connell, a principal officer who happened to be who standing in for Bible John at the time, got sick of listening to Hank's tales and one day, in front of everyone, took him to task. 'So you know all the famous people in Las Vegas?' he challenged.

But Hank did not even seem disturbed at the disbelieving tone adopted by Connell. 'They were all my pals,' he boldly confirmed.

'Well, you tell me,' Connell demanded, 'if you were doing so well in Las Vegas and were pals with Frank, Dino and all those other celebrities you talk about, what the fuck are you doing working here as a screw in Peterhead?'

Not one bit nonplussed by the PO's scathing attack, Hank looked him straight in the eye. 'Ah, well, that's for me to know and for you to wonder about,' he said, leaning against the wall and looking confidently back at his interrogator.

'No! I don't need to wonder,' Connell replied, poking Hank in the chest with his finger. 'You see, I *know* – I know what you're doing here.'

Hank's eyes narrowed at this. 'What then?' he said. 'What do you think I'm doing here?'

'You're on the run from the Mafia,' Connell announced triumphantly, obviously enjoying the pantomime as much as the cons. 'You're hiding from the Mob.' He looked at Hank and shook his head, 'Well, you're fucked now because I'm going to phone them up and tell them where you are!' And, with that, he turned round and headed determinedly for his office, his parting shot of 'Right now!' floating back over his shoulder.

But Hank The Yank, a diehard to the end, still kept his end up. 'Aye,' he shouted, 'that's just the sort of dirty trick you would pull. You're nothing but a fucking grass!'

There was another occasion in the tailors' shop when Hank got into hot water with the same PO. This particular incident gives a bit of an insight to the character of both Hank and Connell, who was, once again, standing in for Bible John.

As was his habit, Hank The Yank was once again regaling his opposite number, as well as indirectly informing the listening cons of course, with how he had saved the day, or night as it really was, for the screws' darts team by throwing the winning score that put them into the final of the premier local darts tourney. What gave this story added veracity was the fact that Hank indeed knew how to throw a mean dart and he actually was a mainstay of the screws' team. But PO Connell was also a member of the darts team and, more importantly, he was the team captain.

'Yeah,' Hank laid it on thick, 'down two sets we were when I came on. No problem,' he mimed his darts-throwing technique. 'Three in the bed – no bother for me. The other guy never stood a chance.' Once again he threw invisible darts across the tailors' shop. 'Pop, pop, pop,' he illustrated how the darts went home. 'Won us the match, I did. See if I hadn't been there . . .' He looked around and shook his head. 'We were out of it but now, thanks to me . . .' He looked round the workshop again to make sure he was the centre of attention. 'We're in the final and, with me in the team, the result is a foregone conclusion.' I think he was expecting us to applaud, the way he looked around the shop, barely resisting the urge to take a bow.

However, his boastful speech did not go unremarked, as PO Connell came storming out from his office his face red with anger. 'Right, you!' Connell stepped up to Hank. 'I'm fed up listening to you telling everybody how you won the match. *You* never won the match – *the team won the match*. You only won two games and that doesn't make you the champion.'

'Makes me the best in the team, though.' Hank looked at him smugly. 'Twelve-dart checkout! How many games did *you* win?' He looked around the cons, a knowing smirk on his face. 'I think I take top prize there.'

'Aye, well, if you don't stop bumming about it, you'll take no more prizes, not for my team anyway.' Connell stormed at him. 'It's a darts team I'm running, not a one-man fucking band. I don't need you to win. So any more of this how-I-won-the-match stuff and you're out of it, dropped from the team.'

'Dropped from the team?' Hank looked at Connell and shook his head. 'You won't do that,' he said. 'Not if you want to win the cup.'

'That's it!' Connell exploded. 'You're out! Dropped! We can win without you, you havering idiot! You're out, finished!' He was still shouting as his office door slammed behind him, leaving a slump-shouldered Hank in open-mouthed shock – silenced for once.

But the story did not end there, as we were to discover when we returned to work on the following Monday morning and heard the results of the darts tournament.

'Aye.' Hank had assumed his usual position with his big fat arse against the radiator at the top of the stairs and he was addressing his colleague in a voice you could hear through walls. 'Done it again,' he said. 'I threw some really great darts and won the match with two sets to go. No bother for your old dad!' Once again he launched invisible darts across the room. 'That's two years in a row I've checked out for the winning team.'

We all looked at one another. Connell must have relented and let Hank back in the team. But why then was he stomping about, obviously raging mad about something and totally ignoring the boastful Hank? The mystery was soon explained, however, when word filtered out that Hank had not only joined the other team, he had also thrown the winning darts, securing victory for his new team with Connell and the prison squad having to settle for second prize. We all looked on in silent glee as Connell stormed about the workshop, complaining and finding fault with just about everything in sight. Meanwhile, you couldn't have wiped the smile off Hank's face with a plumber's rasp.

Christ! You couldn't make it up, could you?

One thing was sure about the tailors' shop, though – you never knew the moment when the unexpected would occur. One minute everyone would be quietly working away at their machines then, out of the blue, a fight would erupt. Something as simple as someone using the steam iron out of turn was as good a cause as any. Suddenly there would be a melee round the ironing table and windows would be smashed and water pipes pulled out as murderers and armed robbers fought over the use of the steam iron. The fight would spread as others took advantage of the distraction to settle an old score. One or two of the more excitable cons would join in simply because they were there.

I remember how, in the middle of one fight, Wullie Leitch (more on him later) picked up his sewing machine and, just for the hell of it or maybe for some lingering grudge, heaved it against the large picture windows of the cutting room. The 'glass' however was actually toughened security plastic and the heavy industrial sewing machine rebounded right on to Wullie's head, laying him spark out.

Then the riot squad was spotted charging down the Burma Road but before they arrived upstairs everyone – except Wullie, of course, who was lying sparko on the floor – was working industriously at their machines. No one had seen anything. In fact, everyone had been so engrossed in their work that nobody was even aware that a fight had occurred. And it was amazing how suddenly so many men could all have fitted into the toilet at the moment the 'disturbance' took place. Only the unfortunate, unconscious Wullie was seized upon and borne off in triumph to the Dardanelles, thus justifying the charge of the riot brigade. It was all a bit like being on the set of an old black-and-white western movie, where the entire saloon crowd breaks into battle and five minutes later it is all quiet again.

There were, however, some serious assaults and stabbings that took place during my time in the tailors' shop, but, to my knowledge, there was only one occasion when anyone ever got charged. This was when a serious escape attempt was made from the shop and an officer was stabbed in the back with a large pair of cutting shears. The escape bid failed when the cutting room screw managed to press the alarm bell to summon the riot squad. This time there was no denying something had taken place and I can still remember having to take an extra long step to jump the huge pool of blood on the shop floor when we were all marched away.

Larry Winters, along with three others, was charged with attempted murder but he was the only one found guilty and was sentenced to another fifteen years on top of his lifer. The other guys got off because, as soon as Larry struck the first blow, the other screws dived for cover and didn't see anything after that.

It's maybe worth noting here that another screw was christened that day with the nickname **Shitty Breeks**. I'll leave it the reader to guess why.

5

BRAIN OF BRITAIN, TWO POOFS AND A SCOTTISH RUFFIAN

Once our daily task was complete and things were quiet, it was always time for the games. Some of these games could be fairly educational – for example, naming the capitals of countries or listing makes of cars in alphabetical order, the loser being the one who fails to come up with an answer. The car game in particular often led to vociferous arguments breaking out, which usually meant the abandonment of the game long before we reached Z for Zephyr or Zodiac (just to show you can go right through the alphabet). For instance, someone would say 'Ford Cortina' and that was OK. Then the next contestant would come out with something like 'Ford Cortina 1600' and cause an argument. A Cortina was a Cortina, no nitpicking allowed over engine sizes or we'd go on forever. The frustrated player would loudly disagree, refusing to play on unless his proffered vehicle was accepted. The game usually broke up then.

There were flower lists, airline company lists, film stars, football teams etc. etc. to go through. It was amazing some of the ideas people came up with to amuse themselves. Even the plebeian game of noughts and crosses had its moments in the tailors' shop – it was all part of passing the time.

Mind you, it was hard going sometimes to keep some of the participants happy, especially when they took exception to the sort of question put to them. **The Brain of Britain**, for instance, was a difficult contender to please. Of course, his nickname was inversely proportional to his true mental capacity.

I named the young guy who sat behind me The Brain of Britain because he was so obviously stupid that it was difficult to include him in our games due to the fact that he slowed everything up by very seldom knowing the answer to the most simple and, as they say now, most frequently asked questions. This guy was unbelievable and, at one time, he stated quite categorically that men in Wales had pricks over six foot long. Of course his statement stunned us but he was adamant. 'I'm telling you,' he claimed loudly, 'men from Wales have six-foot-long pricks – I read it in a magazine.'

Of course, he was ridiculed for his statement but nothing would change his mind and finally he was instructed to bring the magazine into work and show us the evidence. Sure enough, the following day he produced a magazine and threw it down on the table in front of us. 'There, read it for yourselves,' he said, adopting a superior tone and flicking the magazine open for us all to see. 'There you are,' he said. 'It's down there in black and white.' We looked at the article and immediately burst out laughing. It turned out that The Brain had read an article informing the reader that whales could have penises up to six foot in length. Somehow or other The Brain had confused the spelling and totally failed to comprehend the difference between Wales and whales. I only relate this story to illustrate the depth of the man's ignorance and stupidity.

One day, we were at our question-and-answer pastime and it was his turn to produce an answer. As quizmaster, it was up to me to ask the question but, being fair and not wanting to embarrass him, I thought long and hard as I wanted to ask him something that would at least give him a half chance of being right. Finally, I came up with a solution – I would ask him something to which the answer was obvious and I even included it in the very words of the question.

'OK,' I said, after few moments' thought. 'Here's your question.' The Brain was already a bundle of nerves, knowing that he was now the centre of attention. 'How many fourteenths are there in an inch?'

'Oh, no!' He shook his head. 'That's not fair. That's mathematics and I don't know anything about them.'

'Come on,' I said to him, 'just think about it. How many fourteenths are there in an inch?'

He bit his lip, squinted, stared at his worktop then gave up. 'I don't know,' he finally said. 'I don't know anything about mathematics.'

'Look,' I tried patiently with him. 'I'll ask you something along the same lines but easier, OK?'

He nodded agreement.

'Right,' I said, 'now think about it before you answer.' He nodded again but still with a hunted look about him as I posed the question. 'How many halves are there in an inch?' I asked – yes, a question as basic as that.

He looked at me suspiciously, obviously suspecting some trick being played on him but finally, hesitantly, he replied, 'Two?'

'Correct!' I congratulated him. 'Now, think again. How many quarters – that is, fourths – are there in an inch?'

He was becoming more confident now and answered fairly quickly. 'Four,' he said, looking a little smug with himself this time.

'Right again,' I told him. Now I was going to give him one last 'easy' go before I went back to the original question. 'How many eighths are there in an inch?' Well, he looked at me, his eyes going funny again as if looking for the trap. 'Come on,' I encouraged him again, 'you know how many halves and how many quarters there are so how many eighths are there?'

After a long, searching pause he finally gave me a reply that was more question than answer. 'Eight?' He looked ready to be told he was wrong.

'Right again!' I nodded my head. 'Now you've got the idea,' I said to him. 'So, once again, I'm going to ask you the original question.' I could see him bracing himself for the ordeal. 'How many fourteenths are there in an inch?'

'There you go again,' he ranted. 'Fucking mathematics! I told you I don't know anything about mathematics, didn't I? Now you've gone and asked me the same question as before!'

I gave up at that. He was just a hopeless case.

Funnily enough I have just remembered a remarkable piece of convoluted calculations The Brain made one day that made me wonder if I had actually misjudged him. The circumstances were these. It was nearing the end of the football season and someone happened to mention that Celtic were certain to win the league that year because they couldn't be overtaken.

Much to my surprise, up spake The Brain. 'Aye, they could,' he ventured boldly. 'They could still be beaten.'

'How's that?' a voice piped up. 'Look at the points they've got.'

I, myself, have absolutely no interest in football so it follows that I haven't the faintest idea of the ramifications of the league table or points system. However The Brain's boldness had caught my interest so I listened to his reply. Of course I cannot recall his exact explanation – in fact, he lost me halfway through – but everyone else listened intently as he spoke with remarkable authority on the football league table.

Now I know I'm making up the figures in this calculation, but The Brain's explanation did go along these lines: 'Celtic are seven points ahead but they've still got four games to go. Now, if Rangers beat Partick Thistle 3-0 and Motherwell lose to Hamilton Academicals 2-1 and then Partick beat Hamilton and score two goals and, if Celtic lose their last four games, Rangers would only need to win their last three games and score six more goals than Celtic to win on goal average.' He sat back at his machine and looked round at everyone's stunned expressions because apparently he was actually correct in his arithmetic.

It just shows you – maybe if someone had noticed The Brain's aptitude for numbers at an earlier age he may well have achieved something better with his life.

Image and reputation were everything in Peterhead, especially amongst the hard men and the 'gangsters'. Any hint of weakness or fallibility of character could destroy a man and make his life a misery. That was why comebacks were made and justified, on the slightest of provocations. In Peterhead, a man had to show he could not be 'bammed up' (made to look stupid or weak) without some form or retribution, usually violent, being sought.

There was one memorable occasion when one of the big names, perhaps in a moment of recklessness, chose to be bold about things. It was **Zenga**, one of the more outrageous poofs. He came upstairs to the security party in the tailors' shop one day and made a point of speaking familiarly to **Boulder**

Heid, a known hard man. Conscious of the many witnesses and keen to maintain his standing in the macho community of PH, Boulder Heid's response was predicable to most of us but obviously came as a shock to Zenga himself.

'Fuck off!' said Boulder Heid, addressing the flouncing Zenga in no uncertain terms. 'Don't you come trying to talk to me, you fucking wee poof!'

But the suspicions of the workforce were already aroused. Why would the brazen Zenga be so bold as to openly approach Boulder Heid and try to engage him in chit-chat? What made him think such a liberty could be taken with impunity? We all looked at one another. Surely not? The unspoken question hung in the air like a High Court indictment.

Slowly, Zenga backed away, sensible enough to curtail his attempt at conversation with the scowling Boulder Heid, at least at close quarters anyway. Visibly hurt, he edged back towards the safety of the stairs before uttering his damning words. 'Oh,' Zenga announced, his voice trembling with emotion, 'so now I'm just a fucking wee poof? Well, it wasn't that last night when you were shagging the arse off me, was it?'

There was a stunned silence at the accusation and all eyes swung to Boulder Heid, expecting some sort of immediate retaliation – violent, verbal or both. Well, we got one but it wasn't what we were expecting. It would seem that Boulder Heid had decided to apply reverse psychology. Zenga wouldn't embarrass him – he would embarrass Zenga!

'Aye!' He looked round the shop with a stupid grin on his face and yelled at his accuser, 'Aye! Ah was right up ye last night! And ye fucking loved it, ye wee cow!' He stood up and made violent pumping motions with his hips. 'Ye fucking loved it!'

'Oh, aye, you were up me all right,' Zenga repeated, positioning himself at the head of the stairs in preparation for a speedy retreat. 'But why don't you tell your pals that while you were shagging me you were giving me a wank?'

'Ye fucking wee bastard!' Boulder Heid leapt to his feet, ready to do murder. But Zenga was too far away and too quick for him and had bolted for the safety of the downstairs workshop to the sound of our raucous laughter.

George Short was a civilian instructor who happened to have a club foot. Naturally this disability, particularly in the unsympathetic world of Peterhead, attracted the nickname **Gimpy** or **The Gimp**. Short was a real dour character and nobody, cons and screws alike, got on with him. A short, red-headed little bastard with the usual redhead's bad-tempered disposition, he didn't like anyone and nobody liked him. Communications between Gimpy and the cons were kept to a minimum and pleasantries . . . well, they were non-existent. You can imagine his surprise, therefore, when, just as we were closing down for the two-day Christmas break, Wullie Leitch greeted him with the words, 'Mr Short, on behalf of myself and all the other lads in the workshop, I'd like to wish you a very merry Christmas.'

Well, you should have seen Gimpy's face light up. He had actually started to extend his hand and smile when Wullie's devastating punchline was delivered. 'And a hop-hop-hoppy New Year.'

Yes, it was cruel but cruelty is a fact of life in jail. And in Peterhead it wasn't just the odd, snide verbal barb you had to put up with – it was whale-sized harpoons launched with all the force of a guided missile. For a fleeting second or so, Gimpy actually thought a con was being nice to him.

It could have made his year. Instead, his face crumpled to a background of uncontrollable laughter, even the screws struggling to hold it in. 'You . . . you fucking Glasgow keelie bastard!' Gimpy exploded and lunged forward, murder in his eyes.

Wullie didn't even put up a struggle as he was carted off to spend Christmas in the Dardanelles. He knew he would still get his Christmas dinner and avoiding the annual visit of the local Salvation Army band would be a bonus.

Actually the annual two-day Christmas break and a further two days off at New Year were the only holidays the cons ever got in Peterhead. There were no Easter weekends, May Days or any other Bank Holidays for us. For Christ's sake, we didn't even get a day off on the Queen's birthday and we were supposed to be her fucking guests! But, as I kept telling the guys and still do, that's life in the tin pail.

By the way, I looked up *keelie* in a Chambers dictionary – 'a Scottish ruffian' was the definition and very apt it was too!

6

THE TALL-TALE OUTLAW AND RAVING RAMPTON RAB

The American film *Groundhog Day* reminded me of life in jail – every morning starts off the same but small variations occur as the day goes on. Certainly the daily routine had to be followed but, like in the film, there was always some quirky diversion or story turning up to interfere with and break the total monotony of the day.

It therefore made sense that, as we spent most of our days in the workshop, it was there that the majority of these diversions took place. It has to be admitted that Peterhead was full of oddball characters and storytellers, including myself of course, and some, or rather most, of the stories were related by masters of the tall tale.

It was always the stories the cons told about themselves, myself included, that gave us the best entertainment and a laugh is always welcome in jail.

One old storyteller was Michael John Burnside, a well-liked prisoner of traveller stock and the last man to be declared an 'outlaw' in Scotland – hence his nickname **The Outlaw**. He was, for the umpteenth time, relating some of his adventures while prowling and plundering the Highlands.

Hyperbole would be a word outwith Mick's vocabulary but it was certainly no stranger to the structure of his stories.

'Aye,' he said, speaking in hushed tones as he related one of his many adventures, 'I had just done the safe in the Oban Bus Depot and was heading for the hills but someone must have seen me and phoned the polis. Och, there must have been a thousand of them oot looking for me that night but I wasn't worried because, once I get into the countryside, that's it – I'm off! No one can find me once I reach the hills. You see,' he said with a knowing nod of his head, 'I know every blade of grass, every rock, tree, bush and burn in the Highlands. It widnae matter if there was a million people oot looking for me, once I hit the hills, I'm safe.'

'You're talking a lot of shite!' announced Walter (**Watty**) Ellis, a man well known for his direct, outspoken opinions.

Now normally this sort of outright, embarrassing accusation, especially in front of witnesses, would be deemed a serious insult and be met with an immediate violent reaction. But Watty was an old prison friend of Mick so the insult was tolerated to the extent that an explanation was required before any action would be considered.

'Oh, a load of shite, is it?' Mick demanded. 'And how dae ye make that out?'

'You just told us that you know every blade of grass, every rock, tree, bush and burn in the Highlands, didn't you?' Watty repeated him word for word, leaving no room for doubt or error about what Mick had said.

'Aye, that's right! That's what I said. And it's a fact too. I know every inch of the Highlands, so I do.'

Everyone sat back and listened in. Watty's wit was well known and we all knew he was going to say something that would devastate Mick's outrageous claim. We didn't have to wait long as Watty looked up from his machine and nodded, as if considering his choice of words. 'How is it then,' he finally said, in the deadpan voice he adopted when putting someone down, 'if you know every blade of grass, rock, tree and burn in the Highlands, you were up to your neck in a swamp when the cops found you?'

One look at Mick's face told a tale on its own. Guilty as charged!

I spoke to Mick a few minutes later and asked him about it. 'Aye,' he said, ruefully shaking his head, 'he's fucking right enough. He knows everything, that bastard.'

'So what happened?' I asked.

'I was getting away,' he told me, 'when I jumped over this dyke, landed in a bog and sunk right up to my neck. No kidding, I thought I was going under and I let oot a roar that the polis would have heard ten miles away. The fucking cops came and pulled me out and the story got into the bloody papers. That's how that bastard Watty knew about it.'

Big Rab, otherwise known as **Raving Rampton Rab**, was well known throughout the jail mainly because of his prowess as a goalkeeper. His manic dives, clear off the ground on to a very rough shale pitch that was underlaid with concrete in places, were so impressive that even the local Highland League team, Peterhead, made enquiries about his date of release. It was a pity Raving Rampton Rab was doing a fifteen-year stretch for manslaughter or he might otherwise have become a local success story on his release from PH. Ah, chance is such a fickle thing.

Another of the tailors' shop stalwarts, Rampton, as his nickname was often abbreviated to, would sit at his machine and regale the rest of us with some improbable tales. Of course it's true that being in jail gives most of the inmates a flying start in the lying department – it's part of life in the nick – but, as I have often said, who cares how outlandish a tale is as long as it is amusing and entertaining? Many of the stories emanating from the inmates of Peterhead can be taken with a pinch of salt (more likely a huge bag) but a well-told tale, however improbable, is always appreciated as it breaks the monotony and helps to while away the time.

One thing about Raving Rampton Rab was that he seemed inordinately proud about having done time in Rampton Lunatic Asylum, which was of course the source of his nickname. I don't know much about the place but its inmates were mentally incapacitated criminals of all sorts, all of whom were sent there for some crazy, insane offence. I'm not aware of the actual details of Rampton's particular crime but his offence was one of manslaughter and he was in there for four years. As a matter of fact, he now found himself in Peterhead for exactly the same sort of crime but I do not want to go into the details of his offence, except to say it was a horrendous affair. One of the weirder aspects of his behaviour was that he walked into a public bar near his home and plonked two human eyeballs on the counter in full view of everyone.

However, although he was originally charged with murder, the Procurator Fiscal offered to reduce Raving Rampton Rab's charge to manslaughter in exchange for a plea of guilty. Mad or not, Raving Rampton Rab promptly accepted the deal and was sentenced to fifteen years – a long sentence for manslaughter, especially when you consider that sentences of around five to eight years were the going rate for that offence at that time. In fact, even guys sentenced to life were only serving round about ten years in those days. So

Raving Rampton Rab's fifteen years was actually equal to a life sentence as it would mean he would have to serve a minimum ten years. The difference, however, was that, from the minute he was sentenced, Rampton had a definite date of release and, when he was released, he would be free and clear. Lifers, on the other hand, wouldn't have a release date to count on and, when they were eventually set free, they would be on licence for the rest of their lives and liable to recall at any time.

None of us understood why Rampton had been given such a good deal when it seemed to us that he had been done almost bang to rights. Most of us concluded that the PF must have thought Rampton would plead insanity – after all, he had a well-documented record in that department. And, with the eyeballs-on-the-bar business, it wouldn't have been difficult for a half-decent QC to convince a jury that Raving Rampton Rab really was round the bend and big time at that!

I had another theory about it, though, that might explain the PF's munificent treatment of Rampton. I don't think they had enough evidence to be certain of obtaining a guilty verdict because, whenever that is the case, they *always* offer a deal. They are not interested in doing the accused any favours by this – all they are worried about is their careers and they definitely don't want to earn a black mark by losing a case. So they do a deal that secures a guilty plea and chalk up another victory on their CV showing how clever they are. I think that, if Rab had had the nerve to refuse the deal and had opted to go to trial on a murder charge, there was every chance he would have walked free from court. But then, placed in that position, I think most accused people would take the deal – something PFs know only too well.

Anyway, back to Raving Rampton Rab and two anecdotes that kind of show he wasn't quite the full shilling.

Somehow the teatime talk turned to records and radios which were still a bit of a novelty in PH in those days. Someone was complaining about loud music disturbing the peace in the hall late at night.

'Noisy?' Rampton joined in. 'You should have heard it in Rampton! It was really loud in there – in fact, you could hardly hear your own records.'

'Oh, aye?' said Watty Ellis, turning to him. 'And how was that?'

'Well, you see, in Rampton, we were only allowed to play our records and radios in one big room.'

'What? Everyone played their things in the same place?'

From the way he grinned around at everyone, with that insane look on his face, we all knew that a story was forthcoming from Rampton.

'Aye,' Rab left no doubt as to what he meant. 'We all had to take our tape decks, record players and radios into this room if we wanted to hear our music. So I would put on my country and western LP and start to listen to it. Next thing some clown would put on their record player or tape and play their sounds. Then somebody else would come in and play his music. So there we all were in the one room and I would be listening to my country and western music, somebody else would be playing pop music and somebody else would like to listen to jazz or some rubbish like that. Then another guy would like to play ballroom dance music or that classical shite. In the end there would be about a dozen of us in there, all playing different sounds. I could hardly hear my own stuff so I would turn it up a wee bit louder, then the guy next to me would turn up his. Next thing everybody is playing their music louder and louder because of all the noisy bastards next to them. No kidding,' he said, emphasising his words with an exasperated shake of his shaven head, 'everybody was playing their music so loud that you would think you were in a fucking madhouse!'

Raving Rampton Rab could never understand the irony of his statement or why we were all rolling about laughing when he said it. He was just pleased to be the centre of attention and sat there grinning crazily at everyone.

Another of Rampton's unconscious gems came to light through the behaviour of a certain Irish screw who used to do the odd shift in the tailors' shop. He had the very irritating and disgusting habit of constantly cracking bubble gum with his lips. This screw would lean against the radiator at the top of the stairs staring blankly at the floor, chewing away like a two-legged bovine, except bovines didn't make loud cracking noises from their mouths.

There was actually a story behind this particular screw's gum-cracking presence in PH. Apparently he had been working in the Maze Prison in Northern Ireland and had upset the cons so much in there that he got an official warning that his name was going on a hit list if he didn't pick up his P45 and leave. Having no other skills to offer and being unable to work in the Prison Service in Northern Ireland, he uprooted his family and transferred to the Scottish Prison Service to work in remote Peterhead, about as far away as he could get from Northern Ireland without actually emigrating. So now we had to suffer his presence and put up with his disgusting gum-cracking sounds.

Crack! Once again the noise snapped out – I don't think he even realised he was doing it.

'Listen to that dirty bastard,' someone said as we sat around a table having our tea break one day. 'He's always making that fucking noise. It's really disgusting, so it is.'

'Aye,' Raving Rampton Rab piped up. 'So it is. And do you know something?'

We all turned to look at Rab, knowing he was going to come out with something crazy.

'Know what?' Watty E. took up the challenge as big Rab straightened up in his chair, wearing the manic grin he adopted whenever he took centre stage.

Once he was sure he had everyone's attention he announced his latest folly. 'My ma used to do that.'

'What? Crack chewing gum, you mean?' Rampton had our attention now.

'Aye.' His head would swivel round to make certain everyone was listening in. 'All day she would go about the house, chewing gum and making that noise. It went right through me, so it did. Aye,' Rampton nodded. 'Crack . . . crack . . . crack. All day long, she would do it. I would shout, "Hey, Ma, stop making that fucking noise!" And she would say,' (here Rampton would adopt what he considered a whining voice), '"What noise, son? I'm not making any noise." "That fucking cracking noise – it's driving me fucking mad, so you better chuck it," I would tell her. No kidding, you couldn't even read the paper for her. Every couple of minutes, just when you were getting to a good bit – crack! It would make me jump.' And Rampton jerked in his chair to impress upon us the devastating effect the noise had on him. 'And see at night, when I was lying in my bed and the house was all quiet? She would be in her room and I could still hear her cracking away at the gum. "Crack! Crack! Crack! Crack!" No kidding, that's all you could hear. So I would shout at her, "Ma, Ma, you're making that noise again." "What noise, son?"' Rab whined. '"Fucking cracking – that's what fucking noise. You better stop it or I'll come in and fucking strangle you!" So,' he informed us, 'it would stop for a while and everything would be nice and quiet when "CRACK!", she would do it again. So I would shout and bawl at her again and tell her to chuck it. Then she would go quiet but I would still be lying there listening for a crack. Ten minutes would pass without a sound and then I would start to wonder if she was all right. Then I would forget about it and start to go to sleep but, just when I was feeling really sleepy, you know, ready to doze off . . . "Crack!"' Rampton almost jerked himself out of his chair. 'She would do it again and waken me up. It was fucking murder.'

'Hold on a minute, Rab,' Watty E. picked up on him. 'There was a very simple way to stop all this cracking, you know.'

'How?' Rab looked at Watty as if he was the one that was crazy. 'How the fuck could I stop it?'

'Quite easy,' Watty told him. 'All you had to do was take the chewing gum off her.'

'Ha, ha,' Rampton laughed out loud, shaking his head at what he obviously considered a ridiculous suggestion. 'How could I do that?' he asked in an astonished tone. 'It was me that gave it to her in the first place.'

We could only look at one another in silence as Rampton Rab grinned insanely at us.

7

THE HAM-HANDED SPY, BALD EAGLE AND A POISON DWARF

You get all sorts of criminals in Peterhead but an international spy was definitely something different. So, when Peter Dorschell was found guilty of spying on the American submarine base in the Holy Loch, it was obvious that he would be sent to Peterhead and we all looked forward to seeing him. It was also axiomatic, in view of his offences, that he would be allocated to the security party and we were all keenly waiting to meet what appeared to be a very interesting person. However, all our expectations were dashed when the bespectacled **Ham-Handed Spy**, Peter Dorschell, finally arrived in PH to begin his seven-year sentence.

In the early seventies, there was a bit of spy-mania in the English press when a couple of guys were accused of giving information away to the dreaded communists. Not to be outdone, it wasn't long before the Scottish law enforcement agencies found a 'spy' of their very own. The unfortunate target of their attentions was a young German national called Peter Dorschell.

There was no question that Peter was a live and kicking version of that great fictional character, Walter Mitty, and was acting out what he supposed was the glamorous, secret life of an international spy. But, in actual fact, he was a really confused man and about as much of a spy and a danger to the United Kingdom as Mickey Mouse was to the security of the USA. Nevertheless, the full force and attention of the police and security agencies took it upon themselves to promote this harmless crank into the realms of international spy-dom.

I don't know why they made such a kerfuffle or went to such lengths to bring a case of spying against Peter. My theory is that they simply forced the case to show their English counterparts that they too were on their guard against the spying menace. It would have been far better and simpler if they had treated him as the crank he undoubtedly was and just kicked Peter out of the country. And, believe me, even *that* would have been more than he deserved.

I dare say some people and undoubtedly the police too would argue that they had caught a dangerous spy in the act. But of course they would have to say that to justify the severity of the action they took against poor old Peter. But just exactly what did Peter spy on and what secrets did he impart to the enemies of our country? That was a question we debated many a day in the tailors' shop and we dissected and trisected every aspect of his case. He was cross-examined by some of the leeriest minds in criminal history – men well used to interrogation techniques both from police and opposing Queen's Counsels in the highest courts in the land. If there had been any hint of Peter being the genuine article – i.e. an international spy – he would have been tripped up all over the place. But no! Peter proved to be a dreamer.

One day he would be on about being a spy, the next day he would be telling us all how he led a mountain rescue team through a snowstorm in the Swiss Alps. He just longed for what he undoubtedly thought was a romantic, adventurous life. He was, as I stated earlier, a real, live Walter Mitty. At one time, he even tried to get me interested in financing an expedition to South Africa where he knew the secret location of a diamond mine. The following day he was laying out his plans for a safari company taking rich Americans out to hunt big game.

He was actually a great source of amusement to us all in Peterhead. We even got great fun listening to his quaint use of the English language. I remember once when he was extolling the virtues of one of the leading pop singers of the time, Dusty Springfield – which goes to show how long ago this all was. He was struggling with his limited English to find the words to adequately describe her attraction to him. Finally, his face contorted with concentration, he come out with, 'Dusty Springfield is . . . What you say . . .?' He held both hands to his chest in a cupping motion, struggling to find the right words. 'She is very manure.'

He gave us another laugh was when he was relating another of his tall tales about how Interpol were searching the world for him. 'They are looking for me here, they are looking for me there, they are looking for me everywhere (he must have read *The Scarlet Pimpernel* at some time or another) but all the time . . .' He looked around at us with a conspiratorial expression. 'All the time . . .' He searched for the elusive metaphor. 'They are on a wild duck hunt.' Well, ten points for trying anyway. He always looked so frustrated when we burst out laughing at him.

So this was the great spy-bust of the century for the Scottish forces of law and order – a throwback adventurer-romantic who could barely speak understandable English. His 'spying' activities amounted to him hanging about the pubs in Greenock, across the River Clyde from the submarine base, and hissing questions at American sailors from the side of his mouth in highly Germanic tones. Questions such as: 'Ven does your unterzeebot zet zail?' 'Vot missiles do you carry?' 'Ver go you next time?' etc. etc. etc.

He was actually an object of fun in the pubs, with the local people calling him the Nazi spy. No doubt one of the things that dammed him in the eyes of the jury was that he admitted to sitting on the hillside overlooking the Kyles of Bute and taking notes whenever he spotted a submarine either coming or going, the timings of which were generally local knowledge anyway. The fact that dozens of other submarine spotters also graced the open hillside to watch the same exciting movements of these sinister vessels was totally ignored by the authorities.

So there was your dangerous international spy, Germany's very own James Bond, openly loitering about the local pubs with his hand at the side of his mouth asking questions that any local resident could have answered and sitting on a hillside along with half of the local populace watching the subs go by. The whole case was simply a West End farce. Come to think of it, it really would have made a great comedy show.

It was the tabloid press that labelled Peter Dorschell the Ham-Handed Spy. In fact the case against him was so ridiculous that the sensible broadsheet press practically ignored the story. But, as any tabloid journalist worth his/her salt will say, 'you should never let the truth stand in the way of a good story.'

Of course, as the old proverb goes, there's no smoke without fire but where was the fire in Peter's case? There is no denying the fact that he approached the Russian Embassy with pictures and plans of the nuclear submarines based in the Holy Loch – this we have to admit. But what was the extent of his 'spying' and did he pose a threat to national security? I think not.

The authorities justified their actions by claiming criminal intent and, to a certain extent, this might be true. However, on closer inspection, it was discovered that the design plans and pictures of the nuclear submarines he offered to the Russians had simply been purchased from WHSmith, the newsagent in Glasgow's Central Station, in the form of boys' books – hardly a state secret then! Which begs the following question: why wasn't WHSmith the newsagent charged with disseminating precisely the same 'secret' information to anyone – Russian, Arab or Hottentot – who happened to wander into their store and pluck the same magazine from the shelves?

Of course, all this was simply ignored by the zealots of the security services who, along with the Scottish police, were so desperate to demonstrate their effectiveness to their English counterparts. Fired by their very own jobsworth mentality, they needed a spy trial and a spy trial they were determined to have. It was just poor Peter's luck to have happened along, playing the wrong game at the wrong time, and, thereby, giving them the case they yearned for.

Seven years for trying to con the Russians with a boys' book on submarines! I would have given the Ham-Handed Spy a medal for sheer audacity.

I met **Bald Eagle**, Alec McRoby, when he was serving a sentence of four years for shoplifting and ended up in the tailors' shop in Peterhead. I know that four years seems to be a severe sentence and, indeed, it is for what is a common crime that would normally attract a sentence measured in days or, at the most, a couple of months, rather than years.

However, in Scotland, if you have a history of the same type of offence, the police, if they feel vindictive enough (and they usually do) or if they think you are up to more than you have actually been done for, will declare that your offence comes under the banner of 'organised crime' and the courts will reflect the seriousness of this by handing down a much longer sentence, as was the case with Alec. But why would a shoplifter, regardless of how long his sentence was, be sent to the penal colony of Peterhead – a place that was stuffed full of violent, psychopathic, knife- and gun-wielding criminals, including murderers and even three or four double murderers?

The answer to this lay in the fact that Alec was one of those diminutive, short-tempered Glaswegians who were given to bouts of extreme violence at the least slight or imagined insult. As a matter of fact, one of his claims to notoriety was that he had once attacked the well-known Glasgow gangster, Arthur Thomson, during an argument at the breakfast hotplate one morning in Barlinnie Prison. Alec had objected to Arthur pushing to the front of the queue and let him know what he thought about it in no uncertain terms. On being told to shut his mouth, the bold Alec unhesitatingly grabbed a huge container of porridge and promptly poured its contents over Arthur's head. The only thing that saved Arthur from serious scalding was the fact that the porridge had developed a thick skin on its surface. This skin remained in one piece and covered Arthur's head and face like a mask, protecting him from serious scalding as the soft hot porridge underneath flowed over it and on to his clothes. Meanwhile Alec continued to berate Arthur, telling him that he was no different from anyone else and should have waited in the queue.

It is from incidents like this that names and reputations are made in prison and news of Alec's action soon spread around the prison world. From then on, people would think twice before picking on the man who attacked Arthur Thomson. Such was Alec's reputation after the porridge incident that Peterhead was designated as the prison to contain him.

So here Alec was in Peterhead doing a four for shoplifting. Mind you, it was shoplifting with a difference! What happened was that, one day, Alec was strolling along the main shopping street in Perth, a quiet rural town, when his eye was taken by a luxurious, expensive, fur-collared coat that took pride of place in a clothier's shop window display. Taking an immediate fancy to this fine piece of apparel, Alec entered the premises and, after a quick reconnaissance, skipped behind a counter and gained entry to the window area through a convenient door. Quickly, he divested the mannequin of the coat, checked his escape was clear and exited the store with the coat draped over his arm.

Unfortunately, Alec was so taken by the coat that the following day he just could not resist putting it on to proudly promenade along the High Street, basking in the admiring glances from the lesser populace. His mistake was to stop to admire himself in the window of the very shop he had stolen the coat from less than twenty-four hours before. An astonished shop assistant spotted him and the coat, being of exclusive design and the only one in the entire city of Perth, was instantly recognised. A quick phone call to the police resulted in Alec's rapid apprehension and a few months later he was sentenced at the High Court in Perth to four years. I'm sure the judge added a bit on for the sheer audacity of the defendant. Anyway, that was how Alec ended up in

Peterhead sitting at a sewing machine along with the worst of Scotland's miscreants.

It seemed, however, that the sentence was having a more severe effect on Alec than he would ever admit to. After he was only a few weeks into his sentence, we began to notice a strange effect on his hair. At first, we thought the prison barber had just made a mess of cutting it but, as the days passed, it became obvious that Alec's proud head of dark curly hair was rapidly falling out. Within two weeks, all that Alec had left was a few lonely clumps of dark hair sticking out from his bald bonce like isolated palm trees on a desert island.

Alopecia was what they said it was – an affliction brought about by damage to the nervous system. And it certainly didn't do Alec's nervous system any favours when he became known as Bald Eagle from then on. I told you, cons are cruel. I do know that, before the end of his sentence, Alec's hair began to grow in again but the damage had been done. Bald Eagle he was and Bald Eagle he would remain.

Poison Dwarfs – that's what the soldiers of the German Army labelled the City of Glasgow's own infantry regiment – The Highland Light Infantry (HLI) – so called because of their generally short stature and renowned ferocity in battle. Of course, a lot of this ferocity was due to the fact that most vertically challenged people generally seem to have a bad temper that is inversely proportional to their size. It was as if they were making a statement along the lines of 'We might be wee but we're not going to be messed about with.' There is an old saying in Glasgow which goes, 'If all the big people were as bad tempered as all the wee people there would be no wee people left.' I have always thought that there is a fair bit of truth in those words.

One day there was an incident in the tailors' shop that demonstrated just how easily these wee people could lose the rag. Needless to say, we always had a fair number of 'wee people' resident in Peterhead and it would be no understatement to say that they made their presence felt in ways that were out of all proportion to their physical size. Poison Dwarfs they were in the HLI and Poison Dwarfs they were in Peterhead.

Wee (this prefix was common to all Poison Dwarfs) Jimmy McCraig was one such **Poison Dwarf**. A mop of dark curly hair above a constantly belligerent expression gave Wee Jimmy a remarkable resemblance to that well-known cartoon character, Dennis the Menace, and he lived up to this appearance too. One time, in the tailors' shop, he was picking a piece of scrap material from the waste bin when a screw – it was **Banana Back**, if I remember correctly – took it upon himself to become all jobsworth-ish. Adopting an authoritative tone of voice, he loudly demanded that Wee Jimmy put the cloth back in the bin.

Wee Jimmy, however, chose to dispute the matter. 'It's only a bit of scrap,' he said. 'I'm taking it back to my peter (cell) to put on my table.' This practice was usually ignored by the screws. As long as you remained within certain limits, a blind eye would normally be turned to prisoners removing small pieces of scrap cloth and using them as tablemats. Owing to the small size of the cell windows in PH, some of the larger pieces could be made into curtains. Of course there was a notice (isn't there always?) stating that no articles or pieces of cloth or clothing could be taken from the workshop under penalty of being placed on governor's report. In practice, there was an unwritten rule that, as long as you did not overstep the mark, it was a case of live and let live.

'You are not allowed to take material back to your cell,' Banana Back pompously informed Wee Jimmy. 'Put that cloth back in the bin or you'll be on report.' Now a threat like this is like waving a red rag to a bull in PH, especially if uttered in front of other cons where a backdown would be seen as a weakness, and Wee Jimmy showed no hesitation in taking up the challenge as he continued to remove the cloth from the bin.

'I told you,' said Wee Jimmy, his face reddening as our attention focused on the byplay, 'it's only a bit of scrap.' He folded the cloth so that he could stuff down the front of his trousers. 'I'm taking it back to my cell.'

'Right, then,' Banana Back announced, 'I'm placing you on report for disobeying an order.'

'What?' Wee Jimmy stared at him, his face contorted with frustration. 'You're putting me on report just for taking a bit of scrap?'

'That's right, McCraig. You are on report.'

Wee Jimmy looked round the shop, aware we were all staring at him and knowing that we were waiting for his response to this challenge.

'Well, fuck you!' he retorted angrily. 'I'm not going on report for that but hang on a minute and I'll give you something worthwhile you can put me on report for.' And, with that, he picked up a metal chair and systematically went round smashing every window in the workshop. When he was done, to loud cheers from the rest of us of course, he calmly placed his chair back in position and turned to a bewildered Banana Back. 'There you are,' he said with satisfaction in his voice. 'Now you've got something you can put me on report for.' And with that he donned his jacket and went to stand at the head of the stairs to wait to be taken to the cells. Those who would escort him there were already racing hotfoot down the Burma Road in answer to the alarm bell.

I can just imagine the governor shaking his head at the stupidity of Banana Back once he heard the details that had led up to the offence. Forty-eight panes of glass shattered and sixty or so men laid off work for two days for the sake of a piece of scrap cloth – I'd like to have heard what the governor said to Banana Back afterwards.

It must also be mentioned that Wee Jimmy went on to consolidate his reputation as a fully-fledged Poison Dwarf when, several years later, whilst serving another sentence in Parkhurst Prison on the Isle of Wight, he kidnapped an assistant governor and held him hostage for two or three days in his own office. I don't recall what his reasons for this action were but I'm willing to bet they were trivial to say the least.

8

A COLOURFUL CONVICT

Most of the cons in Peterhead, by their very nature, could be said to have led colourful lives. But there was this one guy who became, albeit temporarily, quite literally coloured – so much so that he attracted the appellation **Tweety Pie**. Up until earning that nickname, Manny Cohn was simply called Manny. To this day I don't know if he had another first name because I never heard him called anything else. Judging by his name, his long lanky hair, sallow colouring and the dimensions of the super snib that protruded from his face like a veritable wedge of cheese, he was obviously of Jewish descent. However it was equally obvious that, although of Jewish origin, Manny enjoyed none of the prerequisites or privileges which that particular race seemed to attract when they found themselves in reduced circumstances. In other words Manny was a *poor* Jew or maybe even an *abandoned* Jew, considering that, not once in the years I knew him, did he receive a visit or any pastoral care from the local Jewish community of Peterhead – or anywhere else, for that matter.

Personally, irrespective of his undeniably Semitic appearance, I always doubted Manny's lineage and this was reinforced when his younger sibling turned up in PH and proved to be a standard, fair-haired, blue-eyed Anglo Saxon.

Originally serving a four-year sentence for some mad assault case, Manny managed to contract a severe dose of yellow jaundice in Peterhead – this was before the days when the use of needles by the junkies made hepatitis a common ailment in the prisons of Bonnie Scotland. Anyway, because the disease was highly contagious, Manny was taken off to Aberdeen Royal Infirmary (ARI) and installed in a bed there. Once settled in, he checked out the security arrangements around him, noting that he was in a private room and guarded by only one screw. Surprised at this lapse in security, Manny immediately decided that he would never have a better chance of escape and immediately put a plan into motion.

Not a man noted for his subtlety, Manny simply reach out for a heavy, glass bottle of orange juice, supplied courtesy of the prison governor if you don't mind, and promptly whacked his unfortunate guardian over the head with said weapon, immediately rendering said guardian into a state of unconsciousness. Quickly getting himself dressed, Manny then flew the coop through a handy window and disappeared into the distance.

POLICE HUNT CANARY-YELLOW PRISONER!

It made a good headline and, with a description like that, you would have thought that Manny could not possibly get very far. It was no surprise, therefore, that the police confidently informed the newspapers that an early arrest of the brightly coloured fugitive was inevitable. However, this was not to be the case. It seemed that Manny might have taken on more of the attributes of a canary than simply just its colour – he had sprouted wings and flown off to God knows where.

Newspaper reports warned citizens to stay indoors as the press gave out vivid descriptions of the colourful convict, warning of his propensity for violence and advising anyone who spotted him to stay clear and inform the police of any sighting. Reported sightings came thick and fast and it was rumoured that the local Chinese community laid more than one complaint of harassment against an over-zealous constabulary, with innocent waiters being waylaid on their way to work and dragged off to the local nick, before common sense prevailed. However, despite the many sightings and phone calls, Manny still remained at large and the puzzle of his whereabouts deepened.

It wasn't until three days had passed that the mystery was resolved and the miscreant recaptured. Manny, on making his escape from the hospital area, had been savvy enough to realise that he had to get off the streets and lie low until the scream – and his heightened yellow colour – died down a little. The obvious solution to his problem was to find a house to break into, try to get some money and hopefully find clothes to help him change his appearance. Well, he found a house all right and had no bother breaking into it but, once inside the property, his hopes of finding a decent set of clothes were dashed – that is unless he decided to become a drag queen! The house Manny had chosen turned out to be the abode of three working nurses from the very hospital he had just decamped from and, other than dresses, frilly underwear and a couple of spare nurses' uniforms, there was little to offer Manny in the way of a disguise. Despite this, however, Manny felt safe in the house and was loath to leave, knowing that a furore of excitement now abounded in the streets of Aberdeen.

Making the best of the situation Manny decided to settle down, make himself a cup of tea, have a bite to eat and cross each hurdle as it appeared. As it happened, three hurdles appeared all at the one time when, late on in the afternoon, the rattle of door keys alerted Manny to a trio of nurses arriving home from a hard day's work. Quickly rounding up the three young women – but without resorting to any kind of violence, it must be said – Manny explained the situation to them. I dare say the young women must have been terrified but, being nurses and no doubt trained in the art of dealing with difficult patients, they handled the situation without becoming hysterical or alarming Manny in any way. In fact, according to Manny, as he reported on his return to PH, the three nurses became quite friendly with him. They all sat in the living room, chatting away and watching TV together as they followed the news of his escape and the progress of the subsequent police hunt. 'They all thought it was dead exciting,' Manny told us when he eventually returned to PH. 'They really got to like me and I was getting on great with them. One of them even fancied me,' he assured us.

Well, I really don't know how the girls managed it but, somehow or other, over the space of three days, they convinced Manny that he was their hero and that they were all rooting for him. So successful were they in gaining his confidence that, when one of the girls said she needed to buy some food and cigarettes, Manny felt no concerns about letting her run down to the shops for the goods. But, lo and behold, the fickleness of women! Far from heading for the local grocer's shop as she had promised, the girl had made a beeline straight to the local cop shop instead!

It naturally followed then that, when Manny opened the front door to greet his new-found friend's return, it opened not on to her sweet smiling face but on to the stern faces of a posse of heavily armed policemen who promptly grappled him to the floor before applying a set of manacles, hand and foot, that would have restrained a raging ostrich, never mind a flightless canary. Manhandled out of the house and across the pavement, Manny was unceremoniously slung into the back of a police van and the wire mesh door slammed shut behind him – the canary was caged!

A few months later at the High Court in Aberdeen Manny, already serving a four stretch, had seven years put on top to pay for his brief flight of freedom and the 'kidnapping' of the three nurses. But, as well as this, and infinitely more lasting, on his return to general circulation in Peterhead, he was immediately christened with a nickname fitting for someone who had once been canary yellow himself. From then on, like it or not, he would answer to the nickname of Tweety Pie.

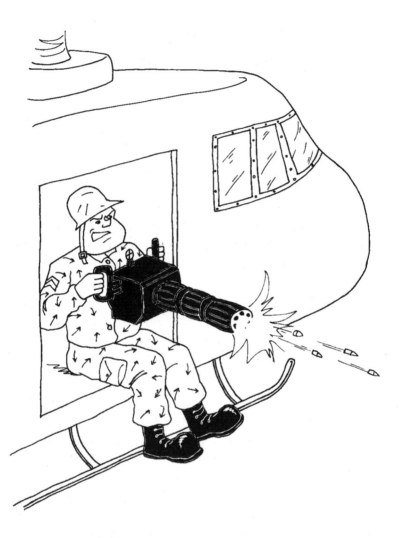

9
BIG BILL VAREY

Big Bill was another welcome addition to the tailors' shop's daily forum. I first spoke to him in A Hall the day before he actually turned up in the shop to work and I knew right away, from the way he replied to a very personal question I put to him, that we would get on well together.

The circumstances were these. One evening, I was walking along the first flat (jail-speak for 'landing') on my way to watch the television when I noticed one of the new arrivals – a big guy, well over six foot in height – leaning on the guardrail looking down at the TV. I think it was *Top the Pops* that was on at the time. Anyway, I took up a position alongside this new fellow, noting how big he was and that, although steely grey-haired, he only looked to be around his late twenties. I had been standing beside this big, square-jawed, tough-looking guy for a few seconds when I became aware of an obnoxious smell invading my nostrils.

My words were totally involuntary, bursting from my lips in a purely vocal reflex. 'Did you just fart there?' I asked him, shaking my head at the odour.

Well, this big guy, arms still folded on the top rail, turned to look at me with a surprised expression on his face. 'I should fucking well hope so, mate!' he told me in a strong Australian accent. 'I surely wouldn't want to stink like this all the bloody time.'

I grinned at him then burst out laughing at the logic of his reply. 'Aye, you've got a point there,' I said, holding out my hand. 'I'm James Crosbie.'

'Bill – Bill Varey.' He held out his own hand and we shook, immediately feeling at ease with each other.

I hadn't read anything about Bill's case in the papers and he had just arrived in PH on the previous day's draft bus from Edinburgh.

It wasn't long before I asked the standard opening question of any new arrival. 'How long you doing then, Bill?'

'Ten stretch,' he told me, going on to add that he had originally been sentenced to fourteen years but had got it reduced to a ten on appeal. Then he reciprocated my question. 'How long you in for yourself?'

'Twenty,' I told him, noting his eyes widening at this information.

I don't doubt that he was wondering what an innocuous-looking guy like me had done to warrant such a lengthy sentence.

'Twenty years,' I confirmed, in case he thought I might have been talking in months.

'Christ, mate,' he said, shaking his head. 'I thought I was doing a big one. What the hell did you get that for?'

'Armed robbery – banks,' I told him, succinctly enough. 'What about yourself?'

'Same as you – held up a couple of banks.'

It turned out that Bill, along with his half-brother, had been travelling the country together in their van carrying out farm-building maintenance work. In the course of their travels, they would spot a small bank in a likely location and, shortly afterwards, return and hold it up. Whenever they came across a suitable bank, Bill would telephone a stepbrother in England, who happened to be a sergeant in the SAS, and ask him to come up and assist them. The stepbrother would arrive and, a day or so later, the trio would hit the bank. Within twenty-four hours, the stepbrother would return to his SAS barracks in Hereford, leaving Bill and his half-brother to carry on with their itinerant farm work. It was a sweet little operation that had the Highland police forces scratching their heads and they would probably have still been scratching their heads if it had not been for an SAS sergeant hundreds of miles away in England.

Apparently, a gang armed with shotguns held up a co-op store in Hereford and made off with the cash. The police immediately threw up roadblocks around the town and began a vehicle stop-and-search exercise. Being on a main road, the best the cops could do was to stop the vehicles, take a quick look at the occupants and check the contents of the boot. If nothing suspicious was found, the car would be quickly waved on.

However, when Bill's stepbrother happened along and was stopped by the police, they found a shotgun in the boot of his car and swiftly pulled him aside. One would have thought that an SAS man found with a weapon, any weapon, within a mile or so of his barracks could easily have explained it away. After all, as I understand things, SAS soldiers are supposed to be 'highly trained' to withstand interrogation – even under torture. Apparently this didn't apply to Bill's stepbrother, though, because, within an hour of being pulled in, without any question of torture or coercion and despite being totally innocent of the co-op robbery, the sergeant broke down and spilled the beans about the robberies he had carried out with Bill and his half-brother in Scotland.

The end result of the stepbrother's confession was a trial in Edinburgh High Court where Bill was sentenced to fourteen years and his young brother got six. The SAS sergeant got off with a wrist-slapping two years and immediate admission to Penninghame House, a 'country club' prison in Dumfriesshire. As a matter of fact the sergeant's minimal two-year stretch paved the way for Bill's original fourteen years being reduced to ten on appeal as disparity in sentences of the co-accused is a valid reason for appeal in Scotland.

Bill was a welcome addition to the tailors' shop work party, having a vast fund of stories to tell. Born in Scotland, Bill had emigrated to Australia with his family when he was a child and it was there that he grew up. However, when he became old enough, Bill decided to return to his homeland and sign up with the Scots Guards – Right Flank, as he always emphasised. He served in the Guards for three years and decided to remain in Scotland after he was honourably discharged at the end of his engagement. It was after his discharge that he teamed up with his half-brother and the pair became itinerant farm-building repair workers, with the occasional bank robbery thrown in to supplement their income. It was a good cover until the SAS stepbrother coughed his lot in Hereford.

It was always great to have a new face in the shop and listen to a few fresh tales. Of course Bill, being so well and far travelled, kept us amused with tales of military derring-do, not to mention his many adventures in the Australian outback as a young teenager. Bill's stories were good but, many a time, his imagination got the better of him and he fell into the trap of gross exaggeration.

The one I remember best was when he was regaling us with some military extravaganza when he was on helicopter patrol on a search-and-destroy mission in some foreign country. He told us that the ground forces had sealed off a group of terrorists in a certain area of the jungle but were having difficulty penetrating the dense bush that hid them. Apparently, his helicopter was ordered to strafe the designated area with a ten-second burst of cannon fire and Bill went to great pains to describe the fire power of his gunship. According to him, the helicopter was fitted with the latest weapons technology and had guns that could cover an area the size of a football field with a grid pattern of bullets only three inches apart. He then compounded his hyperbole by telling us that he fired a ten-second burst into the said ground, thus dispatching the hidden enemy to meet their own particular god.

However, **Wee Jake**, a mathematically minded listener who actually ended up gaining an Open Uni honours degree in mathematics during his sentence, looked sceptically at Bill and raised an enquiring eyebrow. 'You said the guns covered an area about the size of a football pitch?'

'Yes,' Bill replied immediately, not realising the trap that was in the making.

'And you also said that the bullets covered the entire ground area, just three inches apart?'

'That's what I told you,' Bill replied, looking up at his interrogator.

'And you fired a ten-second burst?'

We all looked at each other, sensing that something was brewing in Jake's agile mind – this shooting down of a storyteller (excuse the unintended pun) was the life blood of the tailors' shop party and we looked to Bill for his reply.

'Aye,' he adamantly replied, a little more sharply this time. 'I told you – ten seconds,' he said as he mimed controlling a machine gun and made rat-a-tat noises with his mouth. 'Ten seconds I gave them.' His lips initiated another burst of shells. 'Every living thing in that area below was wiped out.'

'OK,' said Jake, leaning back in his chair and pursing his lips in calculation. 'So we have an area the size of a football field – say, about one-twenty yards by seventy. That would be . . .' He paused as he calculated the sum in his head. 'Eight thousand, four hundred square yards.'

Bill was staring blankly at him, his brow furrowed in thought and no doubt wondering where Jake was going with his musing. He nodded in agreement, still not seeing the pitfall that was heading his way.

'So eight thousand, four hundred square yards getting hit with bullets three inches apart would be eighty-one bullets for each square yard. Multiply that by eight thousand, four hundred and you have a total of . . .' This time Jake resorted to pen and paper to do his calculation. 'Six hundred and eighty thousand, four hundred bullets to cover the whole area.'

By now, Bill was getting a bit red in the face and we were waiting avidly for the punchline. But there was still more to come from our Jake before the full magnitude of Bill's folly was fully exposed.

'A ten-second burst you said, didn't you?' Jake pinned his target with a stare and nodded his head in consideration. He could have ended it there but such is not the way in Peterhead. When you had a man on the ropes, you didn't let go.

'I think I read somewhere,' Jake waxed thoughtful, 'that a machine gun fires at about six hundred rounds a minute, which is ten rounds a second.'

There was a murmur of agreement from the audience at this opinion.

'And you fired a ten-second burst?

Bill nodded, his eyes glaring at Jake as, at last, he tumbled to where the sums were leading.

'So ten seconds of firing at ten rounds a second would add up to over six million bullets you fired into the ground. And, if each bullet weighed even just an ounce, it would mean that, altogether, the total weight you fired must have been around . . .' Out came the pen and paper again. 'Around a hundred and eighty tons. Jesus! What size was the helicopter, Bill?' Jake looked at him enquiringly, as if actually expecting an answer.

Bill clenched his teeth, looked round at our grinning faces, stared at the ground for a few seconds and then, with an unintelligible scream of frustration, launched himself in the direction of Wee Jake. It took about four of us to hold him back from his tormentor but, with all the rolling about and the laughing from the onlookers, Bill soon came to his senses and gave in to being caught out. From now on his stories would be tempered with a bit more common sense and he could consider himself lucky not to be landed with the title Machinegun Bill.

When Bill was released, he travelled down to London and, from there, he went to France and joined the French Foreign Legion. Nothing more was heard from him until a couple of years later when we picked up the morning newspapers and there was a photograph from a bank security camera showing a clear image of him holding a shotgun at his shoulder in the very act of robbing a bank in Lockerbie. He made his getaway in a car that he had parked outside but made the mistake of staying in it too long and was arrested about forty miles away heading down the M6 for London.

With the clear photograph from the camera, Bill had no defence and was sentenced to fourteen years' imprisonment.

The judge made a point of reminding Bill of his previous fourteen-year sentence and stressed that he should not waste his time appealing against his sentence on this occasion.

Within a few weeks, Bill was back in the tailors' shop regaling everyone with entertaining stories about his highly improbable adventures in the French Foreign Legion.

○

10

THE GREAT PETERHEAD HEROIN BUST

This next anecdote actually concerns myself and shows you just how easily a good tale can be generated, no doubt to be told and retold by future generations of cons hell-bent on passing the time.

There are very few pleasures in dreary Peterhead Prison so simple treats take on an added significance and are greatly appreciated. One of the treats that I enjoyed on a regular weekly basis was the purchase and consumption of a tin of sliced peaches which, along with a can of Carnation evaporated milk, I always shared with my old pal Mick Kennedy. And it was this little luxury that one day led to me being challenged by no less than the governor, old **Square Go Gallagher**, in the tailors' shop one day.

It had become my practice to purchase the said goods from the prison canteen on payday and I would stash them away in the back of my cupboard where they would remain untouched until late Saturday afternoon. Opening the Carnation milk tin was never a problem – a quick couple of bashes on the head of a nail with the heel of my shoe would provide the apertures necessary to decant the creamy contents of the tin. However, opening the larger tin of peaches wasn't quite so simple. To achieve this it was necessary to use a tin-opener under the direct supervision of a screw.

As a matter of habit, as well as avoiding the danger of having a tantalisingly open tin of peaches tempting me into immediate gratification, I always delayed the tin-opening ceremony until a few minutes before lockup, which was 4.30 p.m. on weekend days in Peterhead, at which time I would approach a screw and ask to use the tin-opener which was permanently fixed to a corner of the hall desk. Now this tin-opener was a professional model – the type of machine most normally found in a restaurant kitchen where the tin is held under the cutting edge and you turn a handle so that the can is spun round, causing the lid to lift slowly as the blade opens it up.

Well, lockup time was just about due when I approached the desk, tin in hand, mouth already salivating in anticipation of the sweet taste of peach juice that would shortly be mingling with my taste buds. As I approached the desk I held the tin up, letting my actions ask the question for me. The screw obligingly opened his drawer and extracted the handle of the tin-opener and passed it to me, looking on while I fitted it in the slot and held the tin against the blade, making sure I had a good grip on the peaches. Slowly I turned the handle, already 'tasting' the nectar inside the tin.

But then, as the tin lid lifted against the pressure of the blade, I was aware of something odd. Strange, I thought. Being used to a sterile, almost antiseptic atmosphere, I knew that I should already be enjoying the delightful aroma of peach juice titillating my deprived olfactory senses. I looked down as the angle of the lifting lid grew wider and started back in surprise. 'Hey!' I exclaimed, pulling the tin away from the opener and peering inside.

The screw was following my unexpected action with a curious look.

Inside the can, there was no sign of any peaches. All that was visible was a clear plastic bag that seemed to be filled with white powder. 'That's heroin!' I said, wetting my finger before plunging it into the tin and through the plastic bag. My finger came out coated in the white powder and without stopping to think I stuffed it into my mouth. If it had been heroin I would have OD'd immediately. Instead, I found myself spluttering and spitting. 'Salt!' I yelled. 'It's fucking salt!' I looked at the gaping screw then back at the plastic bag. 'How did that get in there?'

By this time, another screw appeared from the office and a couple of the cons were staring over at the activity.

'How did that get in there?' the screw beside me echoed, every bit as puzzled as I was.

'I don't know,' I told him. 'What I want to know is where the fuck are my peaches?'

'Well, there no' in there,' he perceptively replied (clever so they are, these Highland screws).

'I can see that,' I retorted. 'So what about my can of peaches?'

'What about it?' he said back at me.

'I want it – that's what about it. I bought a tin of peaches and all I've got here is a bag of salt!'

'What do you want me to do about it?' he asked.

'Open the canteen,' I pointed at the canteen door just across the hall. 'Open the canteen and replace this tin with a fresh one.'

'Cannae dee 'at, min,' he said, lapsing into the Doric and shaking his head. 'The canteen mannie's no' on shift and Ah dinnae hiv a key.'

'But what about my peaches?' I demanded. 'It's Saturday and I always have my peaches on a Saturday.'

'Aye, weel, ye'll no' hiv them the day, ma mannie. Ye'll jist hiv tae wait fur Monday tae come roon.'

I could barely make out a word he was saying.

Well, I was stuck. There was no way I would get a fresh tin. I knew that, even if there had been a key to the canteen, there was no way **Doric Dumb-bell** would take on the responsibility of issuing me with a replacement tin of peaches.

My earlier euphoria of expectation evaporated as I slowly trod my way up the metal stairs to give Mick the bad news. He was looking at me expectantly when I entered his cell, obviously unaware of the bad tidings I brought with me.

'Mick,' I said, 'I went down to open the peaches but, when I opened the tin, what do you think was in it?' I thought he would never guess in a hundred years what I had found but Mick surprised me.

'A big bag of salt!' he roared at me, grinning all over his face as he opened his cupboard and exposed a bowl of sliced peaches sitting safely inside.

Stunned into silence for a moment, I stared at the peaches then back at Mick. Then I thought about it – Mick was an expert model maker and had, in fact, won both first and third prize in the Scottish Military Modelling Society Competition that very year. No one could be more qualified than him to doctor a tin can. 'You bastard!' I finally got out. 'I've just made a right arse of myself down there over this. I'd better go down and tell them it's OK after all.'

Halfway down the stairs, I was already hearing the rumours spreading. 'Bing's been caught with a bag of smack.' 'Smuggled it in in a tin of peaches.' 'Bing's been done.' 'Aye, bang tae rights, wi' a tin full of heroin.' 'The drug squad's coming in.' The tales were flowing thick and fast as the rumours spread like wildfire. Then I stopped and thought for a few seconds – perhaps I was being a bit hasty here in telling the screws I had been the victim of a prank. After all, I had been genuinely surprised when the contents of the tin had been exposed – no one could have acted like that if they had actually known the tin had been tampered with.

Slow down, I told myself, let's not be too hasty here. Maybe this incident could be turned to advantage. I returned to Mick's cell with a thoughtful expression on my face.

Mick still had a gleeful about him when I entered his cell. 'What did they say?' he chortled, still enjoying my discomfort.

'Nothing,' I told him. 'I didn't let on about it.'

'Oh,' he looked at me curiously. 'Are you not going to tell them then?'

'No,' I said. 'The screw watched me opening that tin and saw that I was genuinely surprised, just as much as he was himself. So I'm going to carry on with it and demand a new tin of peaches on Monday.' It was always good to put one over on the screws and this seemed a golden opportunity to me. I must admit that the expectation of getting one over on the system gave an added piquancy to our usual Saturday treat that weekend.

The following morning, Sunday, I heard the PO calling my name out from the desk and down I went, already anticipating what was going to be said. Sure enough, spread across the desk, like a display of evidence in a courtroom, lay the evidence – one tin lid, one bottom part of the tin, one middle tube part of the tin, one large plastic bag of salt and several pieces of plastic model parts that Mick had used to glue to the inside of the tin so he could reattach the bottom and hide the salt.

The PO looked at me and shook his head. 'What's this, Crosbie?' he sneered. 'Do you think we are all teuchters ['teuchter' is a Scots word for an unsophisticated bumpkin] up here?' He waved disdainfully at the 'evidence'. 'Take that stuff away and bin it. You're lucky you're not on report for this.'

'Here, hold it,' I retorted. 'That stuff there has got nothing to do with me. I bought that tin from the canteen and that was what was in it when I opened it up. I was looking for peaches not a bag of bloody salt.'

At this, the screw who had been overseeing my tin opening efforts spoke up. 'That's right,' he said. 'I was there when Bing opened that tin and I can tell you he was really surprised – same as myself. He never expected to find salt in that tin when he opened it up. As a matter of fact, I'm going to put in a paper about it.'

Now this was good – if the screw 'put in a paper' about it, it meant that he would be writing an official report to the governor supporting my story and strengthening my case for a replacement tin of peaches. The game was swinging my way again. The PO humphed and grumphed at what he obviously considered gross disloyalty but finally had to concede his colleague's right to put in a paper regarding the incident – after all, it wasn't as if the screw was actually going against a fellow officer. I went back upstairs to report my progress to Mick and to await further developments – I knew there certainly would be some.

On the Monday morning, the tailors' workshop was abuzz with the mystery of the doctored tin, the heroin rumours having died away in the light of my remaining in general circulation rather than being dubbed up (locked in your cell) in the Dardanelles, which is what would have happened had there been any truth in the stories.

Then, at about ten o'clock in the morning, the current governor, Square Go Gallagher, appeared on his regular daily visit, like a doctor in a hospital doing morning rounds. I have mentioned this particular governor before. He was well known for his rough-and-ready ways and his attitude on that particular morning was true to form.

'Right, Crosbie,' he said aloud, 'I want a word with you.' And, with that, he walked me down to the half landing between the floors of the workshop, tilted his usual fedora-style hat back on his head and eyed me up like a tough cop in *The Untouchables*.

'What's all this shite about you finding a bag of salt in your fruit tin?' he demanded.

'That's right,' I told him, fully committed now to continue with the scam. 'I opened a tin of peaches and all that was inside it was a big bag of salt. That's all I know.'

'You think we all came up the Clyde on a fucking banana boat?' he said sarcastically. 'A bag of salt in a tin of peaches? Who are you kidding?'

'I'm not kidding anyone,' I told him. 'All I know is that I bought a tin of peaches from the canteen and, instead of getting peaches, all I got was a bag of salt. As far as I'm concerned the canteen owes me a tin of peaches.' I looked him in the eye as indignantly as I could and stood my ground.

Old Square Go stared at me, his eyes crinkled in query. Finally, reluctantly, he came to a decision. 'OK, Crosbie,' he said, nodding his head as he spoke, 'you've worked it this time. I'll authorise a replacement tin on this occasion but don't you think we're stupid. Try a flanker like this again and I'll be attending to you personally,' he warned, determined not to capitulate completely. 'Now fuck off and eat your fucking peaches.'

'Worked it!' I told a delighted Mick. 'He's giving me another tin. We've knocked it off!'

However my joy turned out to be premature. At lunchtime on Monday, I approached the hall PO with a confident smile on my face. 'Right, Mr Knowles,' I said, 'I've come to collect my tin of peaches.'

'Sorry, Bing,' he told me, 'word's come down from the office that you've not to get them.'

'What do you mean?' I demanded. 'Mr Gallagher told me himself that I was to get them.'

'Aye, that's right enough – we heard about that. But Mr Watson, the steward, has countermanded the order. He says you've not to get them.'

'Hey! Wait a minute,' I said. 'Gallagher's the governor – if he says I'm to get my peaches how can this Watson guy overrule him? Surely the governor's the boss?'

'Aye, the governor's the boss but not in financial matters. The prison steward has the final say in anything to do with expenditure and he says you're not to get them.'

Fucked again! I went back to Mick to report on the matter and we sat pondering what to do. 'Tell you what,' I said. 'It might just be a prison canteen but it's no different from any shop in the street. You're supposed to get what you pay for – it's covered by the Consumer Protection Act. If you got a tin full of salt from a shop outside, you wouldn't get fucked about like this, would you?

'Aye but you didn't really get a tin of salt, did you?' Mick pointed out.

'No but they don't actually know that. The suspicious bastards are only surmising that I'm up to something. They can't prove that it was us – well you, I should say – that doctored the tin. Tell you what,' I said, making up my mind, 'I'm putting in a request to see the steward. I want to speak to this Watson guy personally.'

A few days later, I was called out from the work party and marched through the gate in the wire fence that separated the administration building from the rest of the prison to confront Mr Watson. When I think about it now, Watson's behaviour bore distinct parallels with Humphrey Bogart's psychotic reaction towards the portion of missing strawberries in the film *The Caine Mutiny*.

Watson, a typical bespectacled faceless bureaucrat, sat behind his desk with the offending materials spread out accusingly before him – the three pieces of tin can, the bag of salt and the plastic bits and pieces. I must admit it all looked very obvious and I could see Watson's point in refusing to give in to me. But then I had been fooled myself and so had the screw, whose paper to the governor now added valuable teeth to my argument.

Watson sat behind his desk like a High Court judge and I dare say, in his peanut brain, he even felt like one, with the power he held over me. Looking over the top of his thick bifocals he stared me in the eye for a long moment, then looked down at the articles on his desk. Like the megalomaniac he undoubtedly was, Watson waved his hand over the suspect materials and spoke. 'Now can you explain to me, Crosbie, how it could possibly happen that you bought this tin of salt from the prison canteen?'

'Certainly, sir,' I said, launching confidently into my explanation. 'You see, sir, it can actually happen quite easily.'

Watson nodded but his narrowed lips and hooded, suspicious eyes belied his apparently caring attitude as I continued with my tale.

'A man goes into the canteen and buys his weekly supplies, among which is a tin of peaches. He then rushes off to his cell where he has a can that he has already prepared by cutting off the bottom and inserting a bag of salt before resealing the tin again. He grabs up this bogus tin and rushes back down to the canteen, tells the unsuspecting officer (always good to make the screw seem innocent) that he has just realised that he has run out of coffee or tea bags or some other necessity and asks if he could please exchange the tin of fruit for whatever it is he really needs. The canteen officer, being a considerate man and knowing that the prisoner has only just purchased the peaches, obligingly takes the tin back and replaces it on the shelf.'

'Mmmmm,' Watson muttered, his eyes narrowing as he considered my words.

I was not slow to continue with my tale. 'Well, sir,' I resumed, 'a few minutes later, I innocently enter the canteen and, in the course of making my own purchases, I order a tin of peaches. The officer, only doing his job, turns to the shelf and picks up the doctored tin and passes it to me. I take the tin up to my cell and place it safely in my cupboard, keeping it there until Saturday, when I take it down to the desk to open it. It is only then that I discover I have been duped and handed the tampered tin. That is how it can happen, sir.' I maintained a serious expression as I rested my case.

Watson's eyes flickered as he dwelt upon the logic of my theory. I could see it was troubling him but there was actually no way round it. My explanation sounded entirely plausible, and I had the screw's paper to the governor confirming that I had been genuinely shocked when I opened the offending tin. Watson cogitated over my story for a full two silent minutes. It was killing him but he could not come up with any reasonable argument against my theory.

'Do you know how much profit the canteen makes?' he suddenly asked me and the unexpected question took me by surprise. But as it turned out, from his point of view, he couldn't have asked a worse person.

Having been in business myself for years, I could talk away about wholesale prices, mark-ups, profit margins, overheads and retail prices as knowledgably as anyone. So, far from being a stuttering, stammering convict making vague guesses, I launched into an appreciation of the prison canteen's viability as a profit-making organisation.

'Well,' I began, 'to start with you have a captive customer base of around three hundred cons with nowhere else to spend their cash. This must give you a weekly turnover of at least £1000 (remember this was the mid seventies). I would estimate that about half of that goes on tobacco products which have a low profit margin of ten or twelve per cent. However, once you get into sweets and foodstuffs the profit margin must rise to at least around fifty to seventy-five per cent. And, for toothpaste, shampoo and soap sales, the profit margin is even higher still. So, with no wages, rental or power overheads the weekly profit from the canteen must be around . . .'

Watson's eyes were popping and he leapt to his feet, grabbed a ledger and furiously began turning its pages. 'Tea bags!' he shouted, stopping at a page and stabbing it with his finger. 'Tea bags! How much profit do you think we make on tea bags?' I didn't get a chance to reply. He was on to something else – tinned fruit! 'And look at this,' he pointed accusingly and spun the ledger round to me. 'We only make fourteen pence a tin on those sales. Replacing one tin of peaches wipes out the profit on another three.'

Jesus, I thought the man was going to take an apoplectic fit as I nodded my head at appropriate places and tried to look sympathetic. What was actually going through my head as I listened to him ranting was the cost of all the report filling, the screw's time, even the governor's time and now the prison steward himself wasting his own valuable time on it. And all over a tin of peaches!

Finally Watson regained control of himself and sat down at his desk again, twiddling with his fingers and drumming them on the desk. My entire attitude throughout the interview had obviously knocked him totally out of kilter. Eventually, with nowhere to go, he looked up in surrender.

'All right, Crosbie,' he finally conceded, 'on this one occasion I will authorise the replacement of your peaches. Off you go now, back to the hall.' I left his office with a smile and when I looked back I could see him disconsolately disposing of the tin and other parts into the waste basket.

Yes! Done it! I felt a wave of exultation engulf me as I was marched back through the wire fence and down to the halls, the satisfaction from my success all out of proportion to the profit. I had dealt with the devil and come out on top and, with most of the cons now in the know about the scam, it gave all of them a lift when I announced my success and I received a rousing cheer when the canteen officer ceremoniously unlocked his store and presented me with the prize.

It also has to be said that, when the true story inevitably reached the ears of the screws, they took it in good part, acknowledging they had been well and truly conned.

11

TIME BOMBS, HOT PIES AND GUNFIGHTS

I don't want to dwell too much on the terrorist prisoner element in PH but I find it hard to bypass old Malcolm Nicol without a mention. **Malky**, as Malcolm's name was abbreviated to, worked in the tailors' shop along with all the other security men in Peterhead and could always be counted on for a good tale. His stories, more often than not, concerned his activities within his Loyalist group in the east end of Glasgow. One of his better tales was about the time a member of his unit cleverly stashed a batch of explosives in the oven of the local Orange Order hall in Landressy Street, Glasgow. Unfortunately, the catering staff were not informed of this matter and proceeded to light the oven in preparation for heating the evening's traditional repast of hot pies. The resulting explosion blew out the rear wall of the establishment causing the members to think they were under attack from the IRA. Fortunately, the only casualties were the rear wall of the building, the ruined kitchen and a couple of dozen hot Scotch pies.

A thing that always amused me about all the Loyalist organisation members I met in Peterhead was that every one of them claimed to be at least a lieutenant and to have specific jobs within their unit. Malky, for instance, claimed the rank of major and was always telling us about how he was the arms and drill instructor for his section and he would describe stalking unsuspecting hikers through the

Lanarkshire hills for field-craft practice, setting them up for a 'snipe', as Malky put it.

Then we got on to talking about guns in general and I would mention using light machine guns (LMGs), Webley .45 revolvers and .303 Lee Enfields. Someone else would talk about automatics and I mentioned that, at one time, I had three of them, all 7.65s. Talk would then go on to the difference between a 9mm and a .38 and we would get into an argument about them. I noticed that Malky had very little to say about individual types of weapons and wondered at his silence as he was usually a very talkative person.

Eventually, at the end of the tea break, we all drifted away but Malky came after me and sat down by my machine.

'You seem to know a good bit about guns, Bing,' he said, looking at me with an inquisitive squint.

'Aye,' I told him. 'I was in the RAF and then in the army, so I got to fire a good few of them then and I've had a few guns of my own since then.'

'Aye, well, you see,' said Malky, the arms instructor for his local unit, looking at me with a puzzled expression on his face, 'what I've always wanted to know is what does it actually mean when you say .303 or 7.65 and .38. What does all that really mean?'

Jesus! I looked at Malky and wondered just what arms he was qualified to instruct in. 'Well . . .' I tried to explain, 'point 303 is the diameter of the bullet.' I demonstrated on a plastic ruler. 'See,' I said, pointing at the markings on the ruler and counting them off. 'It means that the bullet is three tenths, no hundredths and three thousandths of an inch in diameter.' Not being an arms instructor myself, this was the best way I could describe it.

'But what about a 9mm and a .38,' Malky asked. 'How do you work them out?'

I explained as best as I could, showing him the difference between metric and imperial measurements on the ruler but I could see he wasn't taking it in. When I completed my short dissertation, Malky turned to me and held his thumb and forefinger about three inches apart. 'But how do you tell the length?'

I just gave up. It was obvious to me that anyone instructed by Malky in the art of firearms would be struggling to load a water pistol.

And talking about pistols, the tailors' shop was full of weapons and 'gunfights' were held on an almost daily basis.

At one stage, things got so bad in the tailors' shop that our large cutting shears were taken from us and we were issued with tiny, blunt-nosed little snippers that we could hardly get our fingers through to use properly. It came to the point when a fight hardly caused anyone to lift their heads from their machines. Even these days, years later, I have found myself sitting in a pub when a fight has broken out, with people all around me scrambling wildly to get out of the way while I just sit there in the midst of it all, trying not to spill my pint. But that's enough of the violence. As I said before, I prefer the *Porridge*-type stories of jail. Besides, they're far more entertaining.

The loss of our big scissors, however, cost us an amusing and highly competitive pastime. These scissors were about a foot long, their large handles giving them, if you used your imagination, a pistol grip. With the ruler pocket down the right leg of our overalls as a holster, we had all we needed for fast-draw competitions. You could almost hear the Clint Eastwood music as the 'gunfighters' faced each other down the length of the passage between sewing machines, eyes fixed, fingers quivering over their 'weapons'. It was serious stuff – prestige was at stake.

The signal was given and hands blurred into motion as both went for their guns. Bang! Kapow! Then, just like kids playing cowboys and Indians, the arguments would begin. 'Got you!' 'Bollocks, you were well beat!' 'Fuck you, you're dead!' 'No I'm not, I got you first!' 'You're fucking dead, you cunt!' 'Who are you calling a cunt?' Next thing the 'guns' became knives or bludgeons and they would be rolling about the floor, hacking and stabbing at each other to settle the argument. Then the riot squad would arrive to cart them off, usually via the treatment room, to the Dardanelles. It wasn't really surprising that our substitute 'six shooters' were eventually taken from us – they were causing almost as much damage as the real thing.

Another regular pastime, and this applies to any prison workshop in any prison in the country, was sabotage. In the tailors' shop, burning out the sewing machine motors was the most common form of this type of action. All you had to do was press hard on the foot pedal while preventing the wheel from turning with your hand. This overheated the motor and, in a few minutes, its copper windings would heat up and burn off their insulating varnish, sending acrid-smelling smoke belching from the machine to a background noise of cheering cons. Another burnout! Although it didn't take long for a replacement motor to be fitted, it caused disruption and the perpetrator would enjoy an hour or so of sitting back with a self-satisfied grin on his face.

Arson, too, was attempted at every opportunity, with trying to burn the workshop down a favourite pastime. Simple incendiary devices, like home-made candles, would be hidden away in storerooms or remote corners in the hope that they would burn down and set fire to the workshop a few hours after it had closed for the night, thereby giving the flames time to inflict maximum damage. There had been some success at this in earlier years but, gradually, the cons had run out of hiding places and all they could count on was a temporary flare-up and some superficial damage. But any conflagration, however small, was seen as a moral victory and greeted by cheers from the cons. They knew they were annoying the screws and keeping them, quite literally, on their knees with daily searches for hidden incendiary 'time bombs'.

However, regardless of all entertaining stories, obscure quizzes and inevitable incidents, at the end of every working the day, it was trudge, trudge, trudge back up the Burma Road to be lined up in the yard and searched. We would then have metal detectors run over us before being marched inside to be dubbed up until teatime. One thing was sure, however, *Groundhog Day* was still on the cards for the following day.

However, after six years in the tailors' shop, one of those small changes to routine was just about to kick in for me.

'Crosbie!' The hall PO called me over to his desk one day as I walked into the hall after work. Wondering what I'd done, I went over to him but he just handed me a 'Change of Labour' chitty. 'New job, Crosbie. You start in the stores tomorrow.' And that was it – my days in the tailors' shop were over.

12

DEPUTY DAWG, MAGNUS PYKE AND A STRAWBERRY GATEAU

When I first reported to the stores, I was looking forward to working in an oasis of peace and quiet for a change but I soon found out that I was very much mistaken. Although there were only two cons working in the stores, the administration offices were upstairs. Half a dozen screws worked there and, believe me, the behaviour of one or two of them more than made up for the madcap men of the tailors' shop. Oddly enough, the biggest idiot among them turned out to be the senior PO, known by all and sundry as **Deputy Dawg**.

Of course my colleague and I liked our work or, more accurately, we liked our place of work. The job itself was no bother – our main task was to keep the stores in order and keep the offices upstairs clean and tidy. We were also tasked to make sure that the office staff – the governor and deputy governors, plus all the PO clerical grade screws who worked upstairs – had a continuous flow of tea or coffee to sustain them throughout their day but that was OK because it felt really great just to be able to work without being under any direct supervision.

There were five Principal Officers and a Chief Officer Clerical who worked upstairs, while we toiled away in the basement below. Generally they just left us alone – I suppose to them we were just part of the furniture and of little or no consequence to themselves. As long as we did nothing outrageous, remembered our place and kept them going with tea and coffee, they ignored us – well, all, that is, except for the aforementioned Deputy Dawg.

Deputy Dawg, as I said, was the Senior Principal Officer in the Peterhead administration office when I went to work in the stores. I know that he didn't actually dislike me but he did go out of his way to try to annoy me. I suspect it was because he was one of those screws who have a highly inflated opinion of themselves and expect cons to be very subservient. I was always chatty and spoke to any member of staff just the same way I would address anyone. Now Deputy Dawg was one of those skinny, bald, round-shouldered, bent-backed types who could never, in a month of Sundays, have ended up in a position of power except, of course, in the Prison Service where he could lord it over the lowly prisoners. And he was also, but only because of length of service, second in charge of the office and would be temporarily promoted to chief officer whenever the real chief was off on leave or absent with one of his regular hangovers.

To put it mildly, Deputy Dawg was on a power trip in PH yet he always seemed to be on edge when I was around and he'd order me downstairs as soon as the refreshments were delivered in case I started a conversation with anyone. One of the reasons for this was that once, when a service engineer was fixing the photocopier machine, I took him a cup of tea. Naturally, for me anyway, I started talking to the engineer – it was always nice to meet someone different. Anyway, our conversation got round to who, in the office, had the highest formal qualifications. The engineer reckoned it had to be the chief – what with him sitting there in a gold-braided cap and everything. 'No,' I told him. Then the engineer chose another of the POs who seemed to have a slightly bigger desk than anyone else. 'No, again,' I told him. That was when Deputy Dawg's ears pricked up and he turned on me, knowing immediately what I was leading to.

'Right, Crosbie,' he snapped out, 'that's enough from you! Downstairs right now and get on with your work.'

'It's me!' I told the engineer as Deputy Dawg hustled me away. 'I've got an HNC in Business Studies and I'm only the convict!'

Old Deputy Dawg was livid as I got my words in. Meanwhile, the other screws were looking on at him and grinning, knowing that I was deliberately winding him up – he was never popular with them either – and the engineer just looked up and laughed as I was hustled downstairs by an irate Deputy Dawg.

There was one time, however, when he almost got his own back on me. I got a sudden craving for a nice big strawberry gateau and asked Drew Cullen, in his capacity as canteen purchases officer (they have a title for everyone in the Prison Service), if I could order a gateau through the sundry purchases account.

'If you've got enough money in hand, certainly you can buy a cake,' Drew told me. 'What kind of gateau do you want?'

'Hold it!' Deputy Dawg's voice sounded out. He happened to be acting chief that day and was sitting at the chief's desk trying to look important. 'What's all this about buying a cake?'

Drew told him what was going on, explaining to Deputy Dawg that I had sufficient cash in my pay account to cover the purchase.

But Deputy Dawg began shaking his head. 'No,' he announced, 'you can't buy a gateau, Crosbie. I'm not starting that sort of stuff.'

Then Drew took the trouble to point out, once again, that I had sufficient funds in my account and told him that he didn't mind picking up a cake up for me.

'No! It's not on.' Deputy Dawg was firm. 'If he gets a cake, everybody else will want one,' he claimed.

'Everyone else won't want one,' I argued. 'And, anyway, what if they did? We're supposed to be allowed to buy anything that's not a prohibited item.'

'I'm not having my officers running up and down to the shops getting cakes for you lot so forget it.'

At this point, Drew spoke up again in my favour. 'But I don't mind, Donald,' he repeated. 'Besides I've got to go down to the cash and carry anyway for the rest of the sundry purchases.'

'Here!' Deputy Dawg tapped the two silver PO's buttons on his epaulette, a habit he acquired when he decided he wanted to pull rank. 'What do you think these are, Drew? Snowdrops? If I say there's no cake, then there's no cake.'

Drew looked at me and shook his head. 'He's the boss, Bing,' he told me. 'If he says no, then that's it. Sorry.'

'Bastard!' I muttered at Deputy Dawg, who was now clapping his hands like a child at my disappointment as I made my way downstairs.

A few days later, however, a rather distraught disciplinary chief officer came into the storeroom in a really agitated state. He was known as **Magnus Pyke** because, like the scientist and TV presenter of that name, he had a propensity to make wild gesticulations when he spoke to anyone and, when he entered the storeroom, his arms were windmilling all over the place. 'Crosbie! Crosbie!' he started off excitedly. 'They've got to be found. We have to find them or the whole jail will be turned over.'

'Find what?' I asked, having no idea what he was talking about.

'The goal nets,' Magnus told me. 'The goal nets are missing and, if they're not found, I'll have to tear the jail apart looking for them. You haven't by any chance seen them, have you?' He spread his arms imploringly.

'As a matter of fact I have, Chief,' I said and pointed at a large storage shelf. 'They were dropped in behind that shelf a few days ago.'

'What!' Old Magnus's face looked stunned at first. Then, when I bent under the shelf and pulled out a length of goal netting, he broke into a huge smile of relief. 'Good, good,' he said. 'You've just saved the whole jail from a spin. Thanks a lot, Bing.'

Bing! I was surprised to hear him addressing me so familiarly. So we're pals now, the thought crossed my mind, and I decided to take full advantage of the situation. 'Well, Chief,' I said as I approached him, 'now that I've found your nets, maybe there's something you can do for me.'

'What is it?' He stared at me, hands held out in front of him.

'Is it all right if Drew Cullen lets me buy me a gateau through my sundry purchases?'

'What?' Even old Magnus was surprised at my request.

'A gateau,' I repeated. 'That's all I want. And Drew has already said he doesn't mind getting it for me.'

'Well,' said old Magnus as his arms carved arcs through the air, 'if you've got the money and Drew has no objection, certainly you can buy a gateau.'

Later I went up to the canteen desk and spoke quietly to Drew, explaining what had happened and how the chief had given permission for the cake to be bought. Drew grinned to himself and nodded. 'Right, Bing,' he said, making a note of it. 'Next canteen day, OK?'

Sure enough, a few days later, I was handed a huge gateau full of strawberries and cream – it was one of the best sights I'd seen since coming into the jail. Right away, I cut the cake, putting the largest piece aside so that I could take it down to the wing after work. The remaining piece was cut into three portions, one for me, another for my workmate and a nice-sized bit left over for Drew. It looked even more massive on a small saucer as I took it up to the office along with Drew's tea. Deputy Dawg's desk, when he wasn't acting chief, faced directly on to Drew's place of work. 'Oh, good,' he said when he saw the cake. 'We're getting a bit of cake.'

'You're getting fuck all!' I told him, holding my arm at the elbow and thrusting my fist up at him as Drew made a fuss of smacking his lips and licking some of the cream from his cake.

'But . . . but why?' Deputy Dawg's lower lip was almost trembling as he looked up at me.

'Because you tried to stop me from getting a cake in the first place,' I reminded him. 'That's why.'

A light suddenly dawned in his face as he remembered and then he became all officious. 'That's right,' he said, looking sternly at Drew. 'I told you he wasn't to get a cake. What do you mean by buying one for him directly against my orders?'

Drew looked at him and smiled innocently. 'Oh, the chief rang me up and told me that Bing could get a cake as long as he enough money for it so . . .' He took a long, lingering bite from his cake. 'I bought Bing the cake. And I must say, Donald, it's really tasty.'

'And you're still getting fuck all,' I triumphantly told Deputy Dawg as I made my way back downstairs.

During the whole time I worked in the stores, this sort of petty rivalry went on between us. Deputy Dawg was always trying to put one over on me and he did have a few moments of triumph, too, I have to admit. There was the time I had to take tea and biscuits up to the local visiting committee. I didn't know it at the time but Deputy Dawg was the committee secretary and he was present at the meeting to take down the minutes. Anyway, I entered the office in my usual breezy fashion and was going round the table handing out tea and biscuits when one of the lady members of the committee spoke to me.

'You're Crosbie, aren't you?' she asked me.

'Yes, that's me,' I answered, not in the least intimidated by the high heid yins of the prison business – I always spoke in a friendly and open fashion. 'I'm James Crosbie.'

'And I believe you recently passed your HNC exams with very good results,' said the lady, nodding in approval.

'Yes, that's right,' I answered, full of confidence. 'Business Studies – and I passed three of the five subjects with distinction.'

'Yes, so I understand,' she told me, approvingly. 'I'm actually doing the same course myself just now so I hope I do as well as you.'

'Oh, I'm sure you will,' I told her. 'As long as you read the books and do a bit of studying, you'll pass the exams all right.' We exchanged another word or two then I went back to my downstairs haven to enjoy a cup of tea myself.

However, almost a week later, Deputy Dawg was downstairs shredding some papers when he held a page of notes up and gave me a wicked grin.

'What's that?' I asked him, curious at his behaviour. 'Minutes,' he told me. 'Minutes from the last meeting of the local visiting committee and you should see what they had to say about you.'

Of course my interest was aroused and I wanted to know what had been said. 'Come on then,' I said to him, 'let's see then. What was it they said?'

'I'm not supposed to let a prisoner read them,' Deputy Dawg told me, looking surreptitiously around, 'but, seeing as it's you, I'll give you a quick look.' Then he passed me the handwritten minutes of the meeting.

I don't remember the exact words but, according to the minutes, what had happened was that a committee member had expressed a desire to speak to a murderer, a robber and a confidence trickster. I was very surprised, to say the least, and more than a little annoyed to read in the minutes that I had been identified as the con man.

'Bastards!' I said with feeling. 'Chatting away to me like old pals and all the time taking me for a conman. I'm going to see the governor about this.'

The governor at that time was a Mr Dingwall, whom I got on quite well with. The following morning, I made a point of speaking to him when I delivered his usual morning tea. 'Mr Dingwall,' I began, 'you remember when that visiting committee was here about a week ago and I was speaking to them?'

'Of course, Crosbie,' Dingwall looked at me curiously.

'Well, I have to say, sir,' I told him in a disapproving tone, 'I am very disappointed to find that I was presented to them as a conman.'

'What on earth are you talking about, Crosbie?' asked the governor sitting back in his chair and looking at me as I repeated what Deputy Dawg had shown me in the minutes about the murderer, the robber and the conman. I ended by telling him that I was very upset at being portrayed as a conman. 'I'm a bank robber, not a conman, sir,' I told him. 'I'm not the sort of person that pretends to be your friend then sneaks up and robs you.'

'Wait a minute, Crosbie. You're objecting to be called a conman but you don't mind being called a bank robber?'

'That's right, sir,' I told him. 'If I'm going to steal from you you'll know all about it. There's none of this sleekit pretending to be pals with me. To tell the truth, sir, I'm a bit upset about it.'

'Crosbie,' said old Dingwall slowly shaking his head, 'I haven't the faintest idea what you're talking about.'

I left his office feeling that I had made my point but I was put off a bit by the governor's obvious puzzlement at my accusation.

All became clear when I passed through the office and there was Deputy Dawg grinning all over his face. He had added a fictional extra page to the minutes just to get me biting – and he had succeeded too! I don't want to labour the point about him but there was one incident that gave me the chance to embarrass Deputy Dawg in front of the governor.

The opportunity came about when, one day, we were told to clear out the office loft and burn all the old papers that had accumulated there. We got a good fire going in the patch behind the office and, with Deputy Dawg supervising, proceeded with the job. I spotted a thin blue book being tossed on the fire and grabbed it back. On the cover, in old pen-and-ink writing, it said, 'Convicts Signing for their

Licence on Release'. I opened the book up and the first scrawling signature I saw was that of Oscar Slater, a man who had served nineteen years of a life sentence in bleak Peterhead before he was proven to be totally innocent. Then I turned a few pages and found the signature of Johnny Ramensky, a famous safe-blower, on two or three other pages. This was obviously a historical prison document.

'Throw that book back on the fire!' Deputy Dawg ordered me.

'But this is important,' I told him. 'Oscar Slater's name is in here.'

'Just do what you are told,' Deputy Dawg snapped, grabbing the book and throwing it back into the fire. He turned away and I grabbed the book again before it got damaged. This time I shoved it under my shirt and then carried it back up to the loft and hid it behind a rafter when we went for more papers. The following day, when I went into the governor's office, I acted as if I was a bit nervous. 'Excuse me, sir,' I said, 'when we were burning old papers yesterday, I found a book that I think is important to the prison history.'

'Yes, Crosbie, what about it?'

'Well, sir, I don't want to get myself into any trouble but I stole the book.'

'What do you mean you stole the book?' Dingwall asked, looking a little surprised.

'Well, sir,' I said, acting really nervous, 'Mr Connell was going to burn it. In fact, when I pulled the book from the fire, he took it off me and threw it back into the flames again, even although I had told him it was important.'

'And what did you do with the book?' Dingwall asked me.

'I don't want to get into any trouble over this, sir, but I took it back off the fire and hid it in the loft.'

'And is it still there?' Old Dingwall was really interested now.

'Yes, sir,' I told him. 'I hid it behind a rafter.'

'Come on,' said Dingwall, rising to his feet, 'show me this book.'

And, with me leading the way, we marched through the main office, getting stares from the staff as we passed by.

'Up here,' I said, pulling out the loft ladder and climbing up through the hatch with the governor at my heels. 'Here it is, sir,' I said as I pulled the book from its hiding place and handed it to him.

Excitedly, Dingwall opened the pages and looked at the squiggly inky marks and spidery signatures. 'Yes, yes,' he said, nodding enthusiastically as he perused the pages. 'Thank you, Crosbie – this is just the sort of thing the prison training college museum needs.'

'Yes, sir,' I humbly replied, 'that's what I thought when Mr Connell threw it on the fire.'

Shaking his head, Mr Dingwall went back through the office with the book held high in his hands. He went straight over to Deputy Dawg's desk and waved it right under his nose. 'Mr Connell,' he said, 'you are nothing but a bloody idiot!' And with that he marched away.

Later on Deputy Dawg came downstairs looking really annoyed. 'You done that deliberately,' he accused me, proving that he actually did have a spark of intelligence. Incidentally, the book did indeed end up in the museum at the prison training college in Polmont Young Offenders' Institute where, I was told by Mr Dingwall, they leave it open at different pages from week to week. But, to tell the truth, I'm sorry I didn't keep the book for myself now.

13

CHOCOLATE BARS, WHITE DEATH AND CURRIED COFFEE

The stores job made a big difference for me. Overnight, instead of having to line up and wait in the windswept, freezing yard every morning before being marched off down the Burma Road, I was able to walk unescorted up to the office block at the top end of the prison. And, instead of sitting in front of a sewing machine every morning, I found myself making a cup of tea or coffee and having a read at the screws' morning paper. It was just like having a real job.

There were two of us cons who worked the stores job and, of course, as in any job concerning stocks of food and other useful commodities, there were always little fiddles going on. 'Liberating' coffee and tea almost goes without saying and piercing a pencil-sized hole in the corner of every sugar sack so we could drain off a kilo or so for ourselves were amongst the perks we enjoyed. It was also good to dip into the governor's special supply of biscuits that was kept for hospitality purposes. All in all, it was a nice little job and it made life that little bit more bearable in barren PH.

But it was when I was helping Drew Cullen fill out the weekly hall canteen orders that I stumbled upon a nice little fiddle that still brings a smile to my face.

I picked up a box of Milky Ways from the shelf and was about to load it on the trolley when I noticed that it was past its sell-by date. I pointed this out to Drew, knowing that there was no way any con in PH would accept goods that were not in perfect condition. Selling out-of-date goods was clearly against the law and these hardened criminals, being mostly a contrary bunch anyway, were the quickest to complain at any breach of their rights. They just loved to be in a position where they could righteously complain and would indignantly point out to the canteen screw that he was breaking the law. And here was an ideal opportunity to do just that as the evidence was clearly printed on each and every Milky Way. It would have been a fait accompli for the cons if the canteen screw even attempted to flog the flawed bars and a flood of outraged petitions would soon be winging their way to the office of the Secretary of State. Being well aware of this, Drew Cullen put the box aside and we continued to fill out the order.

Once the canteen orders had been loaded on to the trolleys, I asked Drew what he intended to do with the out-of-date box, pointing out that there was no way its contents could be sold, at least not through the prison canteen. He thought for a moment and then, knowing I was keen on a sweetie or two, he asked me to make him an offer. Hmm, I thought, forty-eight bars of chocolate – they would really go down well. I knew the chocolate bars were no good to Drew so I chanced my arm and made what even I thought was a ridiculous offer. 'Fifty pence,' I said. 'That's all they're worth and no one else would take them anyway.'

He gave me an old-fashioned look for a second or two. 'Is that as high as you'll go?' he asked.

'Hey, Drew,' I pointed out, 'no one else will buy them and they'll only end up being thrown out. So it's fifty pence or nothing.' (Remember we're talking twenty-five years ago when fifty pence would have got you two pints of beer.)

'OK,' Drew nodded, 'you can have them but I don't want to hear about you flogging them off to the other cons.'

'No chance,' I told him, 'they'll keep me going for a good few weeks.'

'Right,' Drew said as he put out his hand, 'it's a deal.'

I was happy enough – fifty pence for forty-eight bars of chocolate – a treasure in Peterhead. Later on, I was lying on top of my bunk when an idea occurred to me and the more I thought about it the better it seemed. Next day, under the pretext of straightening out the shelves, I went through the boxes of sweets and chocolate checking their sell-by dates. Once I found the boxes that were going to be out of date soonest, I shoved a few of them right to the back of the shelf, hiding them behind the more recently acquired stock. Every week I would check up on my secret hoard, making sure that my chosen boxes remained well out of sight. Eventually, when the box passed its sell-by date, I would 'discover' the out-of-date stock and find myself with another sweet little bargain.

It was a good little fiddle and the sweets tasted all the better for having been wangled out of the stores.

I would describe **White Death** a 'nearly nickname' and I relate this short anecdote to illustrate how a bit of judicial intervention can prevent a title sticking as long as the nicknamee takes appropriate action. Drew Cullen, the same screw as in my last story, was aware of the danger of acquiring a nickname and once had occasion to take immediate action or, as he well knew, he would have been lumbered with the title White Death throughout the rest of his career.

I always got on quite well with Drew and one day he told me how he just escaped by the skin of his teeth from being so labelled. He had been attending a course at Polmont Young Offenders' Institution, which had a section set aside as a prison officers' training college – yes a training college for screws, if you don't mind! He told me that he had been in the shower room one day and found that he had forgotten his personal soap bar. On spying a block of the prison-issue White Windsor, known throughout the service by screws and cons alike as White Death, he decided to use it instead of trekking back to his room for his own soap. On finishing his shower, he was drying himself when the YO prisoner in charge of keeping the place clean entered the shower room looking for his bar of White Death. Drew quite openly told the guy that he had used it and that it was in the shower stall. 'Oh, aye,' said the cleaner, 'that's you, then – White Death.'

'Here!' Drew snapped, smart enough to realise he had to nip this in the bud. 'Less of the White Death nonsense!' he warned the lad. 'The name's Drew and don't you forget it.' And, underlining his authority, he told the guy that he would end up back in the sewing shop if he ever heard the name directed at him again. A threat like that would have meant nothing to most guys, the story being too good a piece of gossip not to spread it around, but this con must have been worried that Drew would indeed get him the sack from his cushy number so he kept quiet about the soap. But there's no doubt it was only Drew's timely warning that prevented the nickname White Death sticking to him forever.

I know I have already mentioned **Red Alert** but, as this next incident occurred in a different workplace, I think it suits the chronology of the book if I bring him up again in the office anecdotes.

Baby-faced Red Alert got himself appointed to run the stores office in PH and I honestly do not think a worse choice could have been made. Of course it must be remembered that many a prison officer gets placed in a job simply to remove him from direct contact with the general prison population. It didn't really matter whether a particular screw was entirely capable of doing the job competently or not – as long as he was hidden away and not causing embarrassing situations or being ridiculed by the cons, the other screws were happy. A perfect case in point was making Red Alert the full-time stores officer – a man-management blunder if ever there was one.

One of the ancillary duties Red Alert was responsible for was maintaining the stock of tea and coffee for the governor, his visitors and the rest of the staff in the main office area. The actual preparing and delivery of these refreshments was of course delegated to one of the inmate storemen and, at the time in question, that was moi.

Buying the coffee for the staff break was what they called a local purchase, the money being paid directly by the prison's financial controller whenever Red Alert ordered a catering-sized container of Nescafe Instant from a local retailer. Of course this cash purchase was entered in a ledger and its consumption closely monitored, mainly, I suspect, to make sure that we cons were not stealing too much of it for ourselves. However, because a record was kept, it was easy to see how long a 500-gram container normally lasted.

Red Alert hadn't been too long in the job when he became concerned about how quickly the coffee seemed to be getting used up. One of the reasons for this was what he considered to be the excessive quantities of coffee being consumed by his immediate boss, the chief officer clerical, who appeared to be addicted to the beverage, demanding that a fresh cup of coffee was always at hand. Every half hour or so, when Red Alert saw yet another cup of coffee being borne upstairs, he would complain and, at least once a day, he would get out his book to check the date the coffee had been purchased.

One morning, I took up the chief's first cup and put it on his desk. I had just turned away when he took a deep swallow of his favourite brew and immediately spluttered and spat the mouthful all over his desk. 'Fucking curry!' he shouted at me. 'What are you trying to do, Crosbie? Poison me?' The chief was really angry, glaring at me as if I had deliberately contaminated his coffee with curry.

I convinced him I knew nothing about it and went downstairs to make a fresh brew. It was then that I inspected the contents of the bowl where, to prevent it being nicked (as if!), limited quantities of coffee were decanted and discovered that the granules had been liberally dosed with curry powder. I immediately thought of **Scooter Turner**, a con who had come up to the stores the day before to pick up some rations for the kitchen. He had asked me to fill a small jar with some coffee for himself but, due to Red Alert's recent complaints, I had to knock him back. Working in the kitchen, Scooter would have easy access to curry powder and it would have been sweet revenge for him to adulterate the coffee that was in the bowl. Of course, when I challenged him, Scooter denied all knowledge – well, he would, wouldn't he? Anyway, he got the blame and was barred from coming up to the stores again.

It was a couple of days later when we were preparing the weekly issue of stores for the kitchen – this was the only time we cons were allowed into the storeroom – and I reached up for a tin of curry powder and noticed that the lid was loose. Then, when I looked inside the tin, I saw the paper seal had been broken and folded back. I knew that Red Alert was the only person with access to the locked spice cupboard so everything immediately became clear to me and I marched into his office.

'I know who put the curry in the Chief's coffee,' I announced.

'Oh?' Red Alert looked up at me all innocent looking and asked, 'Who was it then?'

'I can't name names,' I told him. 'In my position, it would cause me all sorts of trouble. But what I will say is that he is a dirty low-life bastard, a scumbag of a man who was prepared to see an innocent guy get into trouble and just sit back and ignore it. He is the lowest of the low – lower than any guy in this jail – and, if it wouldn't cause so much trouble, I'd boot him right up the arse.'

Red Alert's face was crimson as he sat behind his desk listening to me as I slagged him something terrible and there wasn't a thing he could do about it. I enjoyed letting him know what I thought of him but, just then, I didn't realise how thick the man really was.

One of the main responsibilities of the stores officer was to make certain that the correct amount of food was delivered to the jail kitchen on a regular weekly basis. To do this, the entitlement was calculated by way of filling out a 'Ration Sheet' and, needless to say, the figures arrived at were a constant source of contention between the cook, **Tom Soya**, and the incumbent stores officer – in this case, Red

Alert. Stores were kept on a very tight rein but the Ration Sheet was actually a very accurate method of calculating the correct amount of food due. All you really had to be capable of doing was simple arithmetic to get the figures right but therein lay the flaw – unfortunately, Red Alert was somewhat lacking in the arithmetical department.

Week by week, the arguments emanating from the stores office grew louder and louder and more and more heated as Tom Soya sought to extract more supplies from his counterpart but always angrily storming back to his kitchen empty-handed. But every dog has his day and eventually Tom Soya was to have the last laugh over Red Alert.

The time for the biannual stocktaking exercise came along and, lo and behold, the food ledger showed that stocks were short of most of the items we had in store. Red Alert was distraught – his books should balance if he had been doing his job properly but no, there were discrepancies with most of the supplies in store. I particularly remember the beans, probably because they once again reminded me of Captain Queeg and the missing strawberries incident in the film *The Caine Mutiny*. Try as he would, Red Alert could not reconcile the stock of beans to the amount stated in his ledger. At one stage, he went as far as accusing us cons of stealing the missing beans even though he was the only person to hold keys to the food store.

I know it shouldn't have bothered me but it did and I wanted to know how such a huge catalogue of errors could have been made with such a simple system. This is how I know about the beans – I decided to do my own version of Captain Queeg and got the food ledger out for close examination. I added up the entitlement and figured out the stock in hand. The beans should definitely have been in the store so where had they gone? I knew that the answer lay in the ledger and went over the figures again and again and gradually a faint suspicion grew in my mind. Each tin of beans weighed 1.5 kilos and every week the kitchen was entitled to 4.5 kilos – i.e. three tins of same. Yet each week *four* tins had been entered on the Ration Sheet. Suspicions aroused, I wrote down three 1.5s on a piece of paper and asked Red Alert to add them up. Without hesitation he handed me back his answer – 3.15! Yes, the idiot could not count decimals and, every week, he had been sending an extra 1.5-kilo can of beans to Tom Soya, along with all the other extra rations he had miscalculated.

When I explained the arithmetical error to him, Red Alert went spare, rushing to the cookhouse to demand the return of all the extra food he had sent down. Too late, of course – the food was well used up and Tom Soya, a big smile on his face, had no compunction about reversing their roles and telling Red Alert where to put his demands.

Red Alert was definitely a round peg in a very square hole.

14

BISCUITS, JELLY BUTTOCKS AND A LASHING

There was always a silent war going on between screws and cons in prison and the screws were constantly on the alert for any con trying to put one over on them. For instance, a letter would be slipped under the office door or into the post box informing them that there was a parcel of drugs or other illegal items hidden in this place or that. When this happened, there was not, as you might expect, a rush of zealous prison officers hurrying to find the cache and earn brownie points with the chief. This was because, although these notes appeared several times a year, the fact was that, nine times out of ten, they would turn out to be hoaxes.

Being aware of this, experienced screws would, more often than not, pass the note to a rookie officer and allow him to make the find. Of course, the rookies, to please their superiors, would rush to the hiding place and reach in to grab the prize, unaware that several pairs of eyes, both cons' and screws', would surreptitiously be keeping a close watch on them. The parcel, for indeed there would be a parcel, would always be tucked away behind a pipe or in some awkward, hard-to-reach corner where the screw would have to stretch to grab it. However, instead of being rewarded with the discovery of some illegal substance, the screw would usually find his fingers gripping tightly on to a loosely wrapped bag of human excreta that, hopefully, would have torn open in his grasping hand. The sound of hooting laughter would ring loudly in the victim's ears as he rushed, hand held away from his body, to the washroom – just another wee moral-boosting victory for the cons.

It was all about getting one over on 'them' and every little trick that worked was a victory – a moral boost for us cons that livened up life a little inside. For days, the story would be told and retold throughout the prison and, with every telling, it would become more and more exaggerated as the guys described the screw's reaction, his facial expression and the spreading of the excreta until one would have thought he had immersed himself in a cesspit.

However, normally, it was difficult to catch the screws out, especially the more experienced ones. Usually, no matter what you asked them, they would mull it over in their minds, looking for some ulterior motive, before responding to your request or question. That is why I took great pleasure in deflating **Jelly Buttocks** one day and making him look a fool in front of the chief. The incident happened on the spur of the moment late one afternoon when I was returning to the main prison after finishing my work in the stores.

A couple of weeks earlier the canteen had had a new type of biscuit on sale. They were rum-and-raisin flavour and I had bought a couple and thoroughly enjoyed them. However, the following week when I asked for a repeat order, I found that they were sold out. I asked the canteen officer if I could place a regular weekly order for them and he told me that he couldn't guarantee the purchases officer sending that particular brand down to him. Now the canteen purchases officer happened to be Drew Cullen (he of the near White Death nickname) so, the following morning, I asked Drew if I could buy a full box of the tasty biscuits. He told me that, as long as I had enough money in my canteen account, there would be no problem. A few days later, the biscuits arrived and Mr Cullen handed them to me. I was really looking forward to my treat and couldn't wait to enjoy them along with a nice cup of tea.

Jelly Buttocks was on duty that day, guarding the gate that led down to the main prison blocks. It was only when I spotted him that I realised I could take a bit of a rise out of him with the full box of biscuits. You see, the canteen store was part of my working area and, although I had no access to it, I knew that Jelly Buttocks would be suspicious of my possession of a full box of forty-eight rum-and-raisin chocolate biscuits and probably jump to the conclusion that I had somehow or other stolen them.

On the spur of the moment, I decided to play up to him and, as I approached the gate, I made a crude effort to hide the large packet under my jacket. I saw him eyeing me as I got close and moved my arm forward as if trying to obscure the sight of the huge bulge that stuck out from my side. I could tell from his expression that he had become aware of my move and knew he was going to stop me.

'Right, Crosbie,' he said as he stepped directly in front of me. 'What's that box you've got under your jacket?'

'What?' I asked, looking as guilty as I could. 'What box?'

'Come on,' he said, tugging my jacket open. 'Where did you get this?' He pulled out the box of biscuits.

'Oh, that?' I said, acting shifty. 'I bought them from the canteen. Drew Cullen got them for me.'

Jelly Buttocks was staring at the biscuits, his jowls wobbling as he doubtfully shook his head. 'A whole box?' he said. 'I don't think so, Crosbie.'

'Aye, he did,' I insisted. 'I saved up the money and got a whole box in case the canteen ran out of them again.'

He was still shaking his head. 'Nah,' he told me. 'I think you'd better come with me back to the chief's office'.

'But I bought them,' I told him again. 'Ask Drew Cullen yourself if you don't believe me.'

'Come on, Crosbie,' he commanded, gesturing back at the office block. 'I'll have to report this to the chief.'

'Yes?' said Magnus Pyke, the chief officer discipline, raising an arm as I was pushed into his office on the ground floor.

Jelly Buttocks held out the biscuits as if they were a High Court production. 'Caught Crosbie trying to sneak these through the gate, sir,' he said, putting the biscuits on top of the chief's desk. 'Probably stole them from the canteen store.'

'Oh, aye?' Magnus was clapping his hands together as he looked at the box of biscuits and then up to me. 'So where did you get these, Crosbie?'

'I didn't steal them, sir. I've already explained to him that I got Drew Cullen to buy them for me from my canteen account. I was just taking them down to my cell.'

The weary old chief looked at Jelly Buttocks. 'Is that what he said?'

'He did say something along those lines,' Jelly Buttocks admitted. 'But . . .'

Magnus waved both arms and interrupted him. 'And did you check with Drew?'

'Well, no. I just brought him straight in to you.'

Old Magnus picked up his phone and dialled a number.

'Hullo, Drew,' he said, 'did you buy a box of biscuits for Crosbie today?' He listened for a few seconds before speaking again. 'Right, that's fine, Drew.' He put down the phone and handed me the biscuits. 'Go on, Crosbie, down the hall – and don't eat all of those at once.' Then he threw his arms in the air and looked at Jelly Buttocks. 'You should have checked, you bloody idiot – wasting my time like this.'

'But . . . but . . .' the red-faced Jelly Buttocks spluttered.

'But nothing,' the chief said, waving a weary arm. 'Let Crosbie through the bloody gate. And next time do a bit of common-sense groundwork before you start annoying me.'

Jelly Buttock's face was still red from the chief's words as he waddled along behind me, shaking his head. 'You done that deliberately, Crosbie', he complained. 'You knew I was making a fool of myself and you got me into trouble with the chief.'

I looked at him in 'surprise'. 'What do you mean? I told you Drew bought them for me, didn't I? You're just suspicious of any con – that's your trouble.'

He was still sulking when he let me through the gate, knowing that I would soon be spreading the word of his faux pas. If it wasn't for the fact that Jelly Buttocks was an entirely appropriate name for him, he would have been labelled the **Biscuit Man** from then on.

One of the things we had to do in the stores was to hand out uniforms to any new screws starting on the job. On one particular day, we were expecting three men to call in to collect their kit and other bits and pieces like their rulebooks and batons. When we heard they were upstairs checking in, we quickly laid out our stage.

First of all, we pulled an empty clothing rack out into the centre of the storeroom floor and then George, the other con, removed his shirt and spread-eagled himself across the rack. I then 'tied' his wrists to the upper rail and drew half a dozen red stripes with a marker pen across his back. When we heard the new screws coming downstairs I stood swinging a knotted rope in my hand pretending to be giving George a severe lashing.

'That's six strokes, sir. How many to go?' I addressed the stores screw just as the three men entered the room.

The screw, being just as offbeat as anyone else in Peterhead, looked up from his paperwork and said, 'Oh, just give him one more for luck.'

You should have seen the recruits' faces! One went as white as a sheet, his mouth dropping open at the scene before him. The other two, visibly shocked and lost for words, stood staring at the 'unfortunate' George then turned to look at one another with stunned expressions.

Of course, we couldn't keep it up. Their reaction was just too funny and suddenly we all exploded with laughter. I could see the relief on their faces when they realised it was a joke but the point is – and I still think about it today – not one of those trainee screws raised the least objection to the 'brutality' they had stumbled upon. It certainly makes you wonder what sort of guys they actually were.

Because of things like the freedom to work away unsupervised, the little 'liberating' perks, especially enjoying the occasional box of chocolate from the canteen store, and, probably best of all, the peace and quiet to sit with a cup of coffee and read a newspaper every morning, I enjoyed the stores job – believe me, all these little things made a difference to life in prison and it was almost like being normal again. But, at four o'clock, reality kicked in and it was back down through the gate and into the hurly-burly of A Hall and doing time in the real jail.

15

A-HALL MADNESS WITH SOYA AND SEAGULLS

A Hall held about one hundred men, almost every one of them a villain in the real sense of the word. I say *almost* every one deliberately because there were several men in Peterhead who were actually proven to have been wrongly convicted. Obviously Oscar Slater springs to mind, although he was long before my time. In more recent years, a man named Maurice Swanson was jailed for an armed bank robbery and sentenced to seven years. He protested his innocence throughout his trial but off to jail he went. It was only when another robber was convicted and admitted to carrying out the robbery Maurice had been jailed for that he was finally pardoned and compensated. Then there was Paddy Meehan who received a Queen's pardon and £75,000 compensation after serving seven years for a murder he was totally innocent of.

I throw in these occasional references just to remind you that it is a prison I am writing about and not a madhouse – although madhouse would not be too strong a word to describe some of the goings-on of the residents of Peterhead Penitentiary, to give the place its correct title. It's a fact that some of the things that were done there and the people who did them would not have been out of place in the kind of institution that gave our old friend from the tailors' shop, Raving Rampton Rab, his nickname.

Suffice to say that the war against the boring time didn't just end in the workplace, whether that was the tailors' shop or stores – not by a long shot! The cellblocks, too, had more than their fair share of incidents that kept life interesting and playing practical jokes on one another was only one of the ways we kept ourselves amused.

They say that necessity is the mother of invention. Well, in jail, this proverb undergoes a slight change to become 'necessity is the mother of improvisation'! In Peterhead, due to the obvious shortage of materials, it was necessary to resort to using whatever items, natural or otherwise, we could get our hands on to further some of our time-passing schemes. It makes sense, then, that the ubiquitous seagulls that infested Peterhead were often press-ganged into playing a part in our games. These rooftop rats would sit in line on the apex of every roof, their avaricious, beady eyes raking the ground below, ready to dive-bomb the yard at the least sign of food being available.

One day Joe Polding, nicknamed **The Mallet**, happened to voice his fear of these birds, thus bringing himself to the attention of a well-known practical joker. That evening, a slice of bread was temptingly laid out on a window ledge and, sure enough, within seconds, a beady-eyed seagull swooped down on it, only to find itself snared by a loop of string around its legs and stuffed inside a pillowcase.

Always a sociable person, Joe allowed himself to be lured away by the promise of a cup of tea and a biscuit in a pal's cell along the landing. Making sure he was well settled with his snack, our prankster stole into Joe's cell and quickly perched the seagull inside a cupboard, knowing from experience that, in the darkness and surrounded by alien sounds, the frightened bird would sit still and remain quiet. But he also knew that, after nine o'clock, by which time we were all locked up and the bedlam of 'recreation time' had died away, the seagull would start to move around a little.

At first, Joe ignored the small sounds, probably putting them down to wind noise and draughts but, as the gull started moving around more, he was forced to rise and investigate the source of the strange noises. You can imagine his surprise when, on opening the cupboard door, a huge seagull leapt out at him, screeching loudly and frantically flapping its five-foot wingspan in the confines of the tiny cell. We could all tell when this happened because the noisy seagull screeches and hysterical human screams emanating from Joe's cell were loud enough to wake the dead. Needless to say, the rest of the populace were convulsed in fits of laughter!

Another trick that utilised the seagull population for our amusement was to get a new lad from the cookhouse to carry a tray of bread across the open exercise yard to C Hall. Any con who knew the ropes would throw a heavy cover over the bread, hiding it away from the greedy eyes of the ever-present seagulls. The unwary novice, however, would step boldly out into the yard and get about three yards before a snowstorm of screaming gulls swooped on him, every one of them fighting furiously for a slice of his uncovered bread. Next thing the board would fly up in the air and the terrified con would bolt for the door, white as a sheet and shaking in terror.

There were other tricks we used to play with seagulls too – like gluing tin lids on to their feet and letting them fly off to paddle and clank about on the slates of the roof. Then there was the ubiquitous Watty Ellis. He was famed for fitting a herring gull out with a top hat, bow tie and a little waistcoat, making it undoubtedly the best-dressed seagull on the east coast. And, many a time, we'd be watching a TV programme only for it to be interrupted by a large, squawking gull being thrown into the audience, causing a mild panic on the ground floor of the wing. All these incidents gave us a laugh and helped to while the time away.

Food was always a problem in PH. Put it this way, the cook wasn't called Tom Soya for nothing. Forget about the recommended fifteen per cent mix of soya added to the meat. In **Tom Soya**'s case, it was fifteen per cent of meat added to the soya. More often than not, a meat pie contained no meat at all and Tom Soya relied on gravy salt to flavour and disguise his favourite additive. On top of this, his menu for the week, certainly during the years I spent there, remained totally unvaried. The same meals were served on the same day, week in week out, without fail. We had hunger strikes, demonstrations, sit-ins and smash-ups over the food in Peterhead – all to no avail. Tom Soya ruled supreme. It wouldn't surprise me in the least if the same meals are still being served on the same days even now. The highlight of the week was always Wednesday lunch which was fish and chips with peas, followed by an individual trifle – that is, if you call plain jelly with a squirt of cream on top a trifle. What are the odds on that still being Wednesday's lunch this week? If I were a bookie they'd be very short indeed.

Tom Soya ruined most of the food he cooked and the only reason he got away with it was because he worked in a prison. At one time, a local charity approached the governor and asked if the kitchen could prepare food for the local pensioners' meals-on-wheels service. With an eye to local public relations, the governor agreed and instructed Tom Soya to prepare the required meals. Upon delivery, however, most of the pensioners declared the food uneatable and, within three days, Soya's contract was terminated.

Then there was the time the health inspector arrived to check out the cleanliness of his kitchen. The inspector asked Tom Soya if there was any sign of mice in his kitchen and was told by the crook – sorry, cook – that there was not one single mouse in the place. The health inspector must have had a good sense of humour because, when he checked the bread store and found mouse droppings everywhere, he told Tom Soya that he agreed there was not a single mouse in the kitchen. Tom Soya was just breaking into a smug smile when the inspector added sarcastically, 'Because every mouse in here is married and bringing up a large family.'

However, there was the odd occasion when something special to eat turned up – although it must be pointed out that it was never from the kitchen.

It was a rare, mouth-watering treat for some of us when a member of the Burma Road gang or the garden party bagged a rabbit and Barney Noone, otherwise known as **The Gnome**, from the boiler house turned it into a stew. Barney was a legend in his own right – his extraordinary feat of being nominated 'Rat of the Week' three times in succession by the *Daily Record* crime reporter has never been equalled.

The mention of Barney Noone brings to mind another gnome-like con – **Sodjer** (Soldier) Thompson. How he ever attracted this nickname was complete mystery. Sodjer was certainly never in the army because, with a wonky foot and the beginnings of a hump on his back, there would have to have been a State of National Desperation declared before he was ever called to the colours. But, despite his physical deficiencies and mental incapacity, Sodjer and his pal took it upon themselves to mug an elderly female Provvy (Provident) cheque collector and steal her money. The robbery was successfully carried out but, shortly afterwards, Sodjer's accomplice was arrested and charged with the offence. However, he proved to be a stand-up guy and refused to divulge the name of his accomplice. A couple of months later, the case was brought to trial at the High Court in Edinburgh and the woman who had been mugged was asked by the prosecutor if the man in the dock was one of the men who had robbed her. The lady confirmed that the accused was indeed one of her attackers.

'And what about the other man,' the prosecutor continued, 'would you recognise him if you ever saw him again?'

'Oh, yes,' said the woman, 'I would know him anywhere. He was ugly. In fact, he had a face like a monkey.'

'Who are you calling a fucking monkey?' Sodjer's voice rang out loud and clear as he leapt up from his seat in the rear of the public benches. This ill-advised action resulted in his immediate arrest followed, shortly afterwards, by a sentence of four years in jail.

'Nobody's going to call me a fucking monkey and get away with it,' Sodjer would say in stout defence of his action whenever he was questioned about his untimely outburst. Well, it does take all sorts.

16

WATTY'S REVENGE

Mind you, it wasn't all laughs in Peterhead. Tempers were always on a short fuse and even a casual, offhand remark could touch off an immediate outraged reaction. Many a con has been beaten up or stabbed over an ill-advised remark on the result of a football match or some other innocuous subject. Even if hands are shaken and apologies made at the time, loss of face makes a payback almost inevitable. Revenge attacks were normally carried out early in the mornings, the attacker leaving his cell as soon as the screw unlocked his door and hurrying to his victim's abode, hoping to catch him still in bed and half asleep. A quick stab, stab, stab would be dealt out and then the attacker would hurry back to his own cell and carry on as if nothing untoward had happened. The other critical times for this sort of action would be during the evening recreation period or during the rare holidays when guys tended to lie abed during the long days.

One such case was when Jimmy Hasty asked Walter Ellis for a small piece of marquetry veneer to complete a marquetry picture he was working on as a cell hobby. On his request being refused, an angry Jimmy picked up a scrubbing brush and belted **Watty** across the side of his head and hastily departed. Watty did nothing about it at the time and it looked as if he was taking a back seat. However, with Watty being on security due to a twenty-one-year sentence for armed robbery and Jimmy working out a seven stretch in the mat shop, their paths actually seldom crossed. Added to that was the fact that Watty *never* left his cell to engage in any so-called recreational activities in the hall, thereby reducing the chances of them running into one another even further. So, as the months passed, it seemed that the incident with the scrubbing brush had faded from Watty's memory.

One evening, six months or so later, Jimmy was sitting in Howard Watson's cell, along with Mick Kennedy, enjoying a chat and a cup of tea. There was a polite knock at the door and Watty appeared carrying a large basin of boiling water straight out of the immersion heater. Naturally, he totally ignored Jimmy and spoke directly to Howard about the return of some magazine or other. With agreement reached, he turned to leave and unfortunately 'tripped' over the edge of Howard's carpet. Needless to say, Watty lost his balance and lunged forward, 'accidentally' throwing the scalding water straight into the face of an unsuspecting Jimmy.

Oh, what a terrible 'accident'! Jimmy's face peeled like a banana and he collapsed, screaming in agony. Watty was distraught – he ran for help and demanded an ambulance. He was wringing his hands in worry as Jimmy was stretchered off and taken by ambulance to hospital.

Funnily enough, I was one of the few people Watty talked to at any length but no mention of the 'accident' was ever made, even to me. Mind you, Watty always was a very quiet, unobtrusive, deep person who, with very few exceptions, kept himself to himself and took no part in any of the recreational sessions or film nights. The only concession he did make was taking his exercise in the yard. He never missed that and would walk up and down and up and down the same twenty-five-yard track behind the yard goalposts for as long as he was allowed.

He also refused to speak to any prison staff unless it was absolutely unavoidable, referring to them all as warders or turnkeys. At Christmas and New Year, the only holidays and special meals we ever got at PH, Watty would queue up with the rest of the cons and have his tray filled, simply to tip the lot into the garbage bin at the end of the hotplate.

'Keep your fucking Christmas/New Year dinner,' he would tell the baffled screws. 'I just want my normal rations.' Watty was a real quiet rebel in his way.

I was in Watty's cell one evening when the governor of the time pushed open the door and stepped inside. Now this particular governor, **Square Go Gallagher**, a nickname he had earned earlier in his career by challenging borstal boys to a 'square go' in the boxing ring, had always been a bit of a maverick. Accompanied by his chief officer escort, he'd swagger about the jail wearing an old Columbo-style raincoat and a trilby hat on his head, looking like a newspaper reporter straight from the *Daily Planet*. He looked rough and he talked rough, seeming to consider himself a man of the world and in touch with the mood and men of the prison.

'Right,' he said, tipping his hat back on his head and looking down at Watty, who remained seated on his bed. 'What's all this shite about you never leaving your cell or going down on rec'?' he demanded. 'How comes you sit up here farting about with your bits of wood and paint and never join in?'

I was sitting watching Watty, wondering what he would say to this. I didn't have long to wait.

'Who the fuck told you to come in here?' Watty demanded. 'This is my cell. I fucking live in here so don't you come barging in annoying me. If you want to talk to me, call me up and speak to me in your office. Now fuck off!'

'Aye,' said Gallagher, not in the least put out by Watty's outburst. 'You know you're fucking lucky to even be in the jail. You should have been hung years ago!'

'Oh, aye,' retorted Watty. 'Hung, should I? And what for, might I ask?'

'That taxi driver,' Gallagher said, referring to an old case of Watty's where he had been tried for murder at the Glasgow High Court and was handed a not proven verdict. 'You shot that man,' Gallagher told him. 'Everybody knows you shot him. You're guilty as anything, so you are.'

'Well, let me tell you something, Gallagher,' Watty said, as he rose to his feet and leaned his face close to the governor, 'there's a better chance of you having murdered that taxi driver than me.'

I must admit even I was a bit surprised at this accusation and I wondered what the governor would have to say about it.

'What . . . what . . .' Square Go blustered, at a loss for words. 'What the fuck are you havering about?'

'I got acquitted of that murder,' Watty told him, 'you didn't! Now fuck off and leave me alone.'

Gallagher shook his head as he turned to leave the cell, defeated by the illogical logic of Watty's statement. 'Aye,' he muttered, 'they're right, you know. You *are* fucking crazy.'

But, around this madness, life still went on in Peterhead – after all, the jail held over three hundred prisoners and they weren't all crazy. Most of the men just wanted to put their heads down and get on with doing their time. And you could do that too if you wanted to. No one forced you to join a gang. If you didn't want to get mixed up in jail politics, all you had to do was keep yourself to yourself and mostly you would be left alone to get on with it. I was proof of that.

Mind you, I didn't exactly keep myself to myself – my nature wouldn't allow that as I like to natter, keep track of the jail gossip and have a laugh about things as much as the next man. But I made sure that I didn't get involved with the nutcases or allow myself to become embroiled in any of their incessant plotting and planning. Besides, I could always get myself into plenty of trouble on my own, which was why, before barely a year had passed, I found myself lying in the Dardanelles, staring up at the ceiling wondering how to kill a fly. However, to relate this story, I must take you back to the first year of my sentence.

17

ESCAPE TO THE DARDANELLES

Escape had been uppermost in my mind during that first long year – so much so that I 'escaped' every single night. Honest, they were so real – my dreams I mean. Every night I would find myself wandering about my hometown district of Springburn in Glasgow and, even although I was asleep and dreaming, I knew that I wasn't supposed to be there – it was all so real. So real, in fact, that I actually looked forward to going to bed because I knew that I would soon be out and running about my old haunts again. But every morning I would wake up and find myself still in jail and, if there was ever a time of day in Peterhead when I felt really low, it was first thing in the morning. I still remember pausing every single time I sat on the edge of my bed to pull my shoes on for work and saying to myself, 'You stupid bastard, ending up in here.' This went on for nearly two years until, one day, I suddenly realised it had faded away, just like a whistle in my ear.

However, I did more than just dream about escape. At one stage, I got myself a hacksaw blade – it was smuggled up from Edinburgh in the sole of a training shoe – and I began the long, slow task of cutting through my window bars. A big job when you have to cut through six sections of one-and-a-half-inch square cast metal before tackling the three inch by three-eighths of an inch horizontal steel bars outside. I was up for it anyway and I made a small frame that would hold half a blade and grip it steadily enough for use. Then, with a pal called Jimmy Kyle keeping watch for me, I began my task. In all, it would take six cuts in the cast frame and four cuts in the outside steel bars. A formidable job, even if you had the best of equipment and the freedom to use it openly but a hopeless task for my puny tool and whilst working under the close supervision of the screws.

Is it some kind of blind optimism, or maybe sheer stupidity that spurs people like me on to try the impossible? Whatever it is, I was having a go – trying to 'make one', as they say. My optimism had even led me to prepare a rope to get over the wall. It wasn't a thick rope but it was strong. I tested it by tying it to my bed frame and making a loop I could put my foot through. I then stood up and put my full weight on it and it held. Made from heavy fishing-net material woven four or five ply, with pieces of wood tied into it to provide grips for my hands and feet, theoretically it should have done the job. However, despite my best efforts, its capabilities remained just that – theoretical.

After a week of surreptitious sawing, I had managed to cut through two sections of the cast-iron frame and visions of freedom loomed ahead – so much so that I began planning my disguise for when I got over the wall. Looking back, I realise that I was probably lucky not to have made it over the wall. I've always believed in being bold – no sneaking around and looking suspicious for me. Now, it was well known that, on the odd occasion when someone did manage to get out of PH, the police would put a roadblock on the bridge on the road south – believe me, no one ever went north of Peterhead. I reasoned that the best thing would be to travel openly on a bus but, to do that, I would need a good disguise. I had done similar things before when I was on the run in 1974, being the most wanted man in the UK at the time. What I did then was buy myself a small motorbike and a dark-faced crash helmet. This allowed me freedom of movement and I travelled the roads in this disguise while trying to sort out another bank to hold up.

Don't hide or skulk about – that was my motto. If the police – or anyone else, for that matter – look at you, you want to be instantly dismissed as a suspect. You quite literally do not want anyone to give you a second look. Obviously they would be looking for a white man so I decided I would disguise myself as an Indian or Pakistani. There would be no trouble with clothing – after all, I did work in the tailors' shop. Then, with my face suitably browned and wearing a turban, no one would look twice at me – at least that was my theory.

I got myself three or four of those big, brown, fat, felt marking pens and tried to pour the ink on to a saucer to have a practice go at dying my face. What I didn't realise was that there was actually no liquid ink inside the pens; they were just stuffed full with impregnated felt. I tried to wring one of them out but it was no good – all I got was badly stained fingers. Nothing daunted, I tried spreading the colour on my forehead and it seemed to go on very nicely. Encouraged by this success I proceeded to wipe my face over with the saturated felt until I thought I had covered myself nice and evenly. *Thought* was the right word! When I looked in the mirror again – remember we only had small sixty-watt bulbs in our cells – I almost fainted, then I burst out laughing. I looked like a refugee from the *Black and White Minstrel Show* or maybe a negative panda. My face was stained dark in places but there were large lighter bits and the area around my eyes remained pristine white, the darker colour emphasising the difference in shades.

Coco the Clown didn't have a look in and I spent the rest of that night scrubbing at my face with cold water trying to remove the staining. Jesus, what a job! My face was as red as a baby's bottom with a severe case of nappy rash and I still had dark patches and lines on my face. In the morning I was able to get some hot water and this made a better job of things but I was still getting odd looks from the screws and the other guys when I lined up in the yard for work. Obviously I would have to come up with a better disguise but, in the meanwhile, I would carry on sawing.

Then, one night, I got carried away by the noise of a North Sea storm – a storm that should also have carried away the sound of my enthusiastic efforts. A patrolling screw crept round the corner of the cell block and heard the sound of the saw. Jimmy Kyle should have been sacked! The screw immediately alerted his colleagues inside who rushed my door and I was caught bang to rights – hand on saw, saw biting into metal. In flagrante delicto, as they say in the *News of the World*. Bang to rights in the jail. Captured! Again!! Fuck it!!!

So there I was in the Dardanelles, if you remember, lying on my bed – or I should say my bare wooden platform – staring at the ceiling wondering how to kill a fly. 'He wouldn't hurt a fly.' It's a funny expression, that, isn't it? Well, I would. In fact, I spent hours trying to figure out a way to murder the pest that kept annoying me in my cell. You see, I got twenty-eight days all round for my antics with the saw. That meant twenty-eight days' loss of remission, twenty-eight days' solitary and twenty-eight days' loss of earnings. And that was getting off lightly!

'Attempting to escape' – that was the charge laid against me when I was marched in front of the governor for adjudication. There would appear to be no defence – after all, I was caught with the saw in my hands halfway through the third bar on my cell window. Aha! Not so! You are forgetting the devious criminal mind with which I was endowed. Remember, it takes a clever man to act the fool.

'Not guilty, sir,' I replied to the charge. 'I had no intention of trying to escape.'

'What do you mean not guilty, Crosbie? What were you doing with the hacksaw, then? Engaging in a bit of fretwork? Trying out some sort of new cell hobby perhaps?'

'No, Sir, I cut my cell bars as a protest.'

'What do you mean a protest, Crosbie? What were you protesting about?'

'I was protesting about being held illegally on security,' I replied, trying to sound indignant. 'I'm fed up with being treated like an escapee when, in actual fact, I have never tried to escape. So I sawed my bars to justify being treated as an escapee.'

The governor exchanged a long-suffering look with his chief officer and shook his head. 'Wait a minute, Crosbie,' he said, 'are you trying to tell me that you cut your bars because you thought you should not have been on security?'

'That's right, sir,' I replied. 'But, now that I *have* cut my bars, you are definitely fully entitled to put me on security. I knew I would be caught but at least now I don't have to worry about being treated unfairly any more.'

The governor looked at me and then round the other staff in the orderly room, as if seeking help. Then he fidgeted with his hands, obviously at a loss as to what to do. 'A protest?' He stared hard at me, his eyes crinkled in confusion.

'That is correct, sir,' I assured him. 'I never had the slightest intention of trying to escape.'

Finally, he shook his head in total exasperation. 'Right, Crosbie,' he said decisively, having made up his mind, 'I intended to treat this as a serious escape attempt and remand you until the visiting committee could deal with you. However, in view of what you have just said, I have decided to deal with the matter myself and punish you to the limit of my powers.'

Yes! I felt a wave of relief. I knew the governor's limit was measured in days, whereas the visiting committee could take months of remission from me. Dodging the VC was a victory and I listened happily to the governor's admonishing voice as he told me off before handing out his twenty-eight days all round – that is, twenty-eight days' solitary, twenty-eight days' loss of pay and twenty-eight days' loss of privileges – before my escort marched me off to the cells.

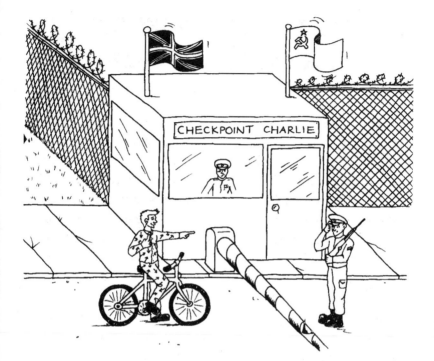

18

PADDY'S ESCAPE TO THE EAST
AND THE FLY-HUNT SAFARI

Solitary in PH is a pretty grim affair. Not only are you on your own in a cold, high-ceilinged cell, there is nothing in the cell except for a stinking plastic pisspot, a solid concrete block for a stool and a fixed wooden platform for your bed. You do have sheets, blankets and a rustling coir mattress but these luxuries are taken from you first thing in the morning and are not returned until eight in the evening. So there you are in solitary with virtually nothing to do and nothing to do it with. The question is, what *do* you find to do? Mainly you just lie on the wooden bed-boards and stare at the ceiling. It's amazing what images you can 'see' up there in the flaking whitewash – maps, faces, animals, clouds and, if you stare long enough, they even seem to move.

Then, every now and again, you can pace round the cell – about twelve average-sized steps take you round the perimeter and four steps each way is as many as you can fit in if you decide to just walk backwards and forwards. Allowing an average of thirty inches or two-and-a-half feet, for each step and considering that there are 5280 feet in a mile, it takes approximately 2000 steps to walk almost exactly one mile. Doing the sums as you go along helps to take your mind off the monotony. I can understand now why they blindfold donkeys on a water wheel.

You can also carry on a conversation with other cell-block exiles but that is hard work because you have to shout to be heard and the reverberating echoes distort the words. But, despite these handicaps, one of the other inmates there, Paddy Meehan – known to his contemporaries as **The User** – managed to tell me the story about an escape he had made from Nottingham Prison some years before when he was serving an eight-year sentence for safe-blowing.

By this time, Paddy had already been down in the cells for the better part of six years, protesting his innocence of a brutal murder for which he had been sentenced to life imprisonment. I don't want to labour on about that particular case but suffice to say that, after seven years of solitary, Paddy was exonerated, released and paid substantial compensation for the miscarriage of justice that had led to him being convicted. However, I was very interested and amused by the story he told me about his escape, in the early sixties, from Nottingham Prison and the steps he took to try and maintain his freedom.

Paddy was aware of another man's plan to escape and he kept a close eye on him, ready to tag along when the bid was made. You see, Paddy was a great long-term planner and he wasn't named The User for nothing. On the day of the escape, according to Paddy that is, he merely followed this other prisoner's tracks out of the jail. It was this calculated manoeuvre that allowed him to claim in his defence when he was eventually recaptured that, technically, he was not the one that 'broke out' of prison. All he did, Paddy claimed, was follow the path made by the other man. However, whether he broke out or not was a moot point – the fact was that he did escape. But his next trick was so unexpected that, even today, it still raises smiles among the criminal fraternity who knew The User well.

Once on the run, Paddy called in one or two old favours and managed to obtain a birth certificate, along with some supportive ID papers. Once armed with these vital documents, he lost no time in applying for an annual passport from a busy Post Office and was soon heading for Dover, where he boarded a cross-channel ferry and disappeared into mainland Europe, his destination East Berlin. Paddy was well educated and spoke fluent German and it was this ability that no doubt weighed heavily in his decision to seek sanctuary in East Germany, safe from the police forces of western Europe. But it must have given a squad of East German frontier guards the shock of their lives when, a few days after his escape, Paddy boldly cycled up to their border post demanding asylum.

To say that the guards were surprised would be an understatement, considering the fact that their days were usually spent preventing people fleeing to the West. Yet here was a crazy, German-speaking Scotsman begging to be allowed in. The puzzled guards permitted him entry but immediately placed him under arrest and escorted him to their headquarters in East Berlin. Once there, he was locked up until he could be properly interrogated, it being practically unheard of for anyone from the free West to escape to the East! Under the circumstances this 'defector' certainly needed further investigation.

Paddy found himself installed in a temporary prison – a former hotel that had been adapted, with bars on the windows and locked and strengthened doors to make it a secure place to hold people such as journalists and minor political troublemakers. Interrogators listened to Paddy's tale about his escape from prison in England and his desire to remain in East Germany but it just didn't make sense to them. Even although they could, and probably did, check his tale against newspaper reports from England regarding the prison break, they remained unconvinced that Paddy was who he claimed to be. As a result of this suspicion, they kept him locked up for almost a year while they pondered over him.

It was only when one of the guards mentioned what he considered to be strange behaviour from his prisoner that Paddy was accepted for what he was. It was the daily, one-hour exercise period that finally turned the tide for him. You see, the other inmates were all first-timers in a prison of any sort and being locked up was sheer torture for them, their only relief being one hour's outside exercise a day. As a result, they were practically tearing the door down when they heard the guards shouting the welcome words, 'Frei Stunde!' ('Free Hour!'), everyday. As soon as their doors swung open, they'd dash out like greyhounds from their traps and, once in the exercise yard, they would brace themselves and draw the fresh air deeply into their lungs, frantically stretching and exercising to get the utmost benefit from their brief hour outside.

Paddy's reaction was somewhat different. When the guard shouted again and entered the cell to see why his prisoner hadn't appeared he would invariably find him in bed.

'What's the weather like?' our bold Paddy would enquire. And, on being informed that it was dull or wet, he would snuggle in and instruct the bemused guard to 'shut the fucking door'.

When the captain in charge of Paddy's interrogation was informed of this strange behaviour, he realised that this could only be the conduct of an old lag and suddenly Paddy was believed.

Shortly afterwards, Paddy was brought up before a tribunal of officers who told him that they were now convinced he was telling them the truth and that he was genuinely seeking asylum. They went on to inform him that asylum would be granted and that he would be supplied with a council house and, in view of his fluent German, he would be employed translating books in the local library. However, they sternly warned him that a close eye would be kept on his behaviour and, if he ever transgressed in any way, he would be sent to prison – a real prison, that is, not the 'hotel' he had recently been held in.

'And you wouldn't like our prisons, Mr Meehan,' he was warned. 'They are not as soft here as your prisons in England. So what is your decision? Do you wish to stay here or do you wish to return to your own country?'

Paddy thought for a few moments then looked at his tribunal. 'I think I'd like to be sent back,' he told them.

He was handed over to British authorities at the infamous border crossing, Checkpoint Charlie, and held in West Berlin until a police escort arrived to take him back to Nottingham Prison. Always one step ahead, once he was back in the jail, Paddy claimed that, as he had been held in custody during his sojourn in East Berlin, his time spent there should count towards his original sentence by the British courts. Believe it or not, they agreed to this. And, when he put forward his claim that he did not actually *break out* of Nottingham so he could only be charged with absconding, they went for that one too. He was well named The User.

Oh, and by the way, several years later, the notorious Russian spy, George Blake, who was serving a sentence of forty-two years, escaped from Wormwood Scrubs Prison in London. Within days, Paddy was laying claims that he had set out the plan whilst being held in East Berlin – definitely a trier and a user to the end, our Paddy.

Other than those basic pastimes of pacing and shouting to a neighbour – if you had one, that is – there was little else to do in the Dardanelles. At least that was the case until I discovered the sport of fly hunting.

One long dreary day I was watching the ceiling, my imagination running wild, when I got my eye on a fly. Yes, there it was, a fly standing upside down on my ceiling, no doubt looking back at me with at least one of its fifty pairs of eyes. The fly just stood there and I just lay there, both of us staring at one another, like a Mexican standoff. I hadn't long finished my dinner and there was an uneaten piece of bread on my tray. Not thinking too much about it I picked up the bread, rolled it into a ball with my fingers and flicked it at the fly. I missed it by just a few inches and was surprised when the insect didn't scoot off. Cheeky bastard, I thought.

Determined to show it who was boss, I got up off my boards, retrieved the bread and flicked it at the fly again. This time I was even closer and again the fly still did not blink as much as one of its hundred eyes. Now I was asking myself if it really was a fly, especially when my third shot landed on the ceiling no more than an eighth of an inch from its head with no reaction whatever. Carefully taking aim, holding the bread in my fingers now instead of flicking it with my thumb, I began a serious attempt at maiming the fly. Sometimes I missed by a fair distance, other times I was so close that I thought I had actually touched it. Still the fly refused to budge. It became a challenge now and I got into the hunt in earnest. Finally success! My piece of bread thudded full on the fly and brought it to the floor.

I was intrigued by the entire episode. Was this a retarded fly without the sense to move out of danger or was it simply disorientated by being upside down on the ceiling? It gave me something to think about and I couldn't wait for another fly to end up on the ceiling. Bits of food left by broken windowpanes should attract more of them, I thought. And so it did. About an hour after baiting my trap, I realised that there were two or three of the little fuckers flying about my cell. I welcomed those flies like long-lost friends – if clouting them with one of my socks could be considered friendly.

Eventually one of the flies headed for what it undoubtedly thought was the safety of the ceiling and I went for my bread ball like a cowboy going for his gun. Up it went. Again . . . again . . . and again. The same thing happened – unless the bread actually touched it, the fly stayed put.

Eureka! I had found my pastime and the sport of fly hunting was born. I became quite skilled at tossing my bread ball – so much so that I would often land slap bang on target first hit. The first time this happened I did a little victory jig round my cell but I soon realised that a first-time kill deprived me of the tension of the stalk. Then, with the hunt over so quickly, I had to wait until I could lure another target into the killing zone. Oh, yes, it was crazy, I know, but it certainly passed the time and, instead of spending twenty-eight days in the Dardanelles, I convinced myself that I was on a four-week fly-hunt safari.

I spread the word to the other guys in the cells and at first they laughed at me and told me to fuck off. (Doesn't the same thing happen to all great innovators?) But, eventually, out of sheer boredom as much as anything else, I suppose, they gave it a try. Soon they too were enjoying the excitement of a fly hunt. Within a couple of days, scores were being kept and boasted about, some guys even keeping the dead flies as trophies to prove their skill.

But holidays in the Dardanelles, just like holidays anywhere else, come to an end. So, with two or three hundred dead flies to my credit, I rolled up my bedding and returned to my cell in A Hall.

19

CLOSET AND BRAZEN TOMPOOFERY

My twenty-eight days in the cells had seen no change in PH. Christ, twenty-eight years had seen no change in the place! Nevertheless, what there was of life had gone on and there was gossip to catch up with. On top of that, it was good to enjoy some human company again so I was glad to sit in with Watty and be brought up to date with what had been going on in my absence.

Nothing out of the usual – half a dozen transfers in and out. **Scruffy Sim** had gone to Bar-L for accumulated visits. **Mac The Knife** had been returned on a lifer-licence recall. There was a rumour that we were going to get lamb chops for dinner in a couple of weeks' time. The new three-month film list was up and looked pretty crap and, of course, there had been a couple of stabbings – one over the use of the tea urn, the other because of a false accusation about some sort of poofery.

It was a rare occurrence in Peterhead – the tompoofery I mean. In all the years I spent there, I can only think of maybe half a dozen occasions where incidents of blatant, outright homosexuality came to light. In the normal course of events, it was statistically inevitable that, every now and again, one or two of the more extrovert gender benders would turn up at Peterhead and unashamedly strut their stuff, taking full advantage of the 'kid in the sweetie shop' syndrome to enjoy several clandestine 'affairs'. But one thing was sure, if anyone did have an 'affair' it was all kept behind closed doors. Well, it would be, wouldn't it?

Occasionally, however, there would an 'accident' that could lead to the unexpected disclosure of a 'face' as a closet homosexual. What happened was this. A young guy arrived in the hall – a round, glowing-faced, bespectacled little fellow with a very definite effeminate air about him. Now this little guy, I don't recall his name, was small even to me and I'm barely five foot eight so, to the towering, six foot three Davie Watson, he must have seemed a veritable midget.

Apparently Davie had managed to sneak the little guy into his cell where, in the unlit shadows, he proceeded to have his hitherto unsuspected wicked way. In mitigation, it's got to be said that the wee fella was a willing partner. However, it so happened that a young, inexperienced screw was supervising the rec' that evening and was patrolling the landing when he heard strange grunts and heavy breathing emanating from Davie's cell. Now an older, more experienced screw would have minded his own business and just walked on by but not this guy. He just had to stick his nose in and, upon opening the door, he discovered two naked men locked in what could only be described as a homosexual embrace – or, as the screw later informally described it, **Davie Doughnut** (his nickname from then on) buried to his balls in the wee guy's behind.

It must be reported here that Davie Doughnut's presence of mind on being caught in this completely comprising situation was admirable. 'Help! Help!' his voice sounded loudly round the landing.

For a moment some of us thought there had been an incident – perhaps an ambush, which was a not uncommon occurrence in PH. But, when the little guy appeared from the darkness of Davie's cell, with a big smile on his face, shirt over his arm and still pulling up his strides, all became clear.

'Help! Help!'? No chance! No one was having any of that.

The situation was viewed so seriously by his associates that I was called in to arbitrate on the matter so they could decide whether or not Davie should be expelled from their company.

I like to think that I was quite open-minded in my appreciation of the situation. 'What harm has Davie actually done? He's still the same guy and it's really nobody's business what he gets up to behind closed doors. If he enjoys a bit of bum, so what?' I argued. 'It doesn't mean he wouldn't stand by you.'

'Aye and you can fuck off too!' I was collectively informed after delivering my considered opinion, which, by the way, I still consider valid.

There was one regular in Peterhead, however, who made no bones about his sexuality and that was **Big Nellie** Drummond who, strangely enough for a person of his inclinations, was well liked and on good terms with most of the 'known' villains and jailbirds of Scotland. In fact, many of them knew him outside and had even worked with him on occasion. During his alternating spells in the free world, Nellie kept his homosexuality well in the closet but, once he was in the jail, he became quite brazen.

Nellie also got on well with the screws whenever he was in Peterhead and, on admission to PH's B Hall, his usual place of residence, he would be put in charge of the stores, the cleaning and the hot plate – all of which he organised with the efficiency of a first-class maître d'hôtel. As a matter of fact, they used to say you could pay off a couple of screws when he came into the hall and resumed his duties. And, as well as this, Nellie would immediately take over the jail bookmaking business, to which he applied the same dedication and efficiency as he did with his daily work, even accepting cash bets from several of the screws.

There are a lot of stories about Nellie and the things he got up to in Peterhead and there's no doubt in my mind that Ronnie Barker's Fletch could have learned a thing or two (two dozen more likely) from him.

Along with the usual tobacco trade, Nellie trafficked in chocolate bars – three for two on a weekly basis – as well as trading in banknotes (25p in the £1 commission) smuggled in from visits. I always thought that, if he had applied himself on the outside half as much as he did when he was inside, Nellie would have been a millionaire in no time. Needless to say, stories about Big Nellie are legendary in the Scottish prison system, especially among the older cons, but I have always considered the two I am about to relate here as among the best.

The story that did the rounds of Peterhead was that a newcomer, a naive young prisoner, made the mistake of going into Nellie's cell to borrow a couple of LP records.

'Oh, aye, sure, son,' Nellie said, inviting the young chap into his cell. 'You'll find a box of them under the bed. Take a look and see if there's anything you like.' Then, as the unsuspecting young man bent low to look under the bed, Nellie suddenly grabbed him round the neck in a half nelson, at the same time ripping off the unfortunate chap's trousers.

Now everyone had heard stories about Nellie having a massive member and personally I can only go on hearsay but rumours were rife – Nellie was BIG! The story goes that as Nellie forced himself upon the attractive young man, gripping him tightly in his favoured half-nelson grip while thrusting away at his rear, the lad was heard to scream, 'Oh, oh, stop it! Stop it! You're hurting my neck!' Strangely enough, after that incident, it was seldom anyone in PH ever had the nerve to complain about having a sore neck.

In the 'good old days', before drugs became the pre-eminent trading commodity in prison, every jail had a bookie and prisoners would bet with tobacco, receiving their winnings in kind. But prisons, harbouring the sort of people they do, meant that the bookie was a target, with nearly everyone trying to put one over on him. One desperado spent hours perfecting the insertion of bread into an empty half-ounce tobacco packet, boldly presenting the finished product to Nellie as his stake on a horse that duly obliged at odds of 3–1.

'Oh, aye,' says Nellie when the trickster appeared. 'You had that bet on the 3–1 shot, didn't you?'

'Aye,' the confident conman held out his hand. 'Makes a change to pick a winner, eh?'

Unperturbed, Nellie looked the man straight in the eye and repeated, '3–1, wasn't it?' before turning away to open his cupboard. 'Right, then, I'll just get you your winnings.'

The beaming 'gambler' could hardly contain himself – no doubt he was already dreaming of an entire weekend puffing away on unlimited roll-ups and probably thinking about swapping a half ounce for a few bars of chocolate to round off his celebrations.

'There you are – that's your stake back,' Nellie said as he handed over the original doctored half-ounce packet. Then, with his face straight as a die, he counted out three thick slices of bread into the shattered prisoner's outstretched hand. 'And, at 3–1, that's your winnings.'

20

SICK PARADE BLUES

Talking about having a sore neck reminded me of the hurdles we had to overcome in the event of reporting sick. Believe me, complaining about any medical ailment was always a problem in Peterhead. The doctor who was there during most of my stay was renowned for his curt, offhand treatment of prisoners. Not exactly a wire brush and Dettol man, Doctor Manson nevertheless seemed to view his panel of prison patients as nothing more than a bunch of skiving malingerers.

When I think back on it now, reporting sick in Peterhead involved you in a catch-22 situation. In a process designed to deter, you were forced to leap out of bed at 6 a.m. and clatter downstairs to the PO's desk to report sick. Once your name had been noted, you were placed on the sick list and, at 7 a.m., immediately after breakfast and come rain, hail or snow, you were marched across the open yard, to sit in a freezing waiting room until the doctor deigned to appear. This is where the catch-22 kicked in – if you were able to get up at dawn, march across the yard and sit in a cold waiting room/cell for a couple of hours, then obviously you couldn't be all that ill in the first place. It was a fortunate patient indeed who left Doctor Manson's surgery with anything more than a couple of paracetamol pills or a note for a day in bed. Fuck me, you needed a two-day bed-down to get over the ordeal of reporting sick!

To say Doctor Manson was insensitive would be like calling the Pope a Catholic. There was this one guy I particularly remember, mostly because it gave us all a laugh. **The Mad Major** (there's one in every jail) had a serious falling-out with Doctor Manson over an incident with his artificial leg. I remember the Major stomping back into the hall one day, moustache bristling, face red in outrage, spluttering and uttering all sorts of threats against the good doctor.

'That Manson's an ignorant, unfeeling bastard!' he announced to all and sundry. 'I'm reporting him to the British Medical Association. He's not treating me like that and getting away with it.'

'Getting away with what?' a voice ventured. 'What did he do to you?'

'What did he do? What did he do?' The Major could barely control himself as he spluttered, red-faced with rage.

By this time, a few guys had tuned into his vocal diversion. 'Aye,' half the listening cons echoed. 'what the fuck did he do?'

'He . . . He . . .' the Major stuttered. 'He tried to make me look stupid. He ridiculed me – the bastard deliberately went out of his way to embarrass me,' he finally got out.

'Aye,' we chorused, all nodding, 'but how? What did he actually do?'

'I went to see him about my leg – the socket was chafing my thigh and I wanted some new padding fitted to ease the pain. Manson told me to take my leg off and show him the worn part. So I got it off and there I was standing on one leg and he said . . .' The Mad Major drew an indignant breath before repeating, 'He said, "Just hop along to the waiting room and I'll call for you." *Just hop along!*' He glared around. 'I'm reporting him to the British Medical Association

– that's what I'm going to do. I'll give that ignorant bastard "Just hop along . . .".'

I must admit he got little support from us as we all burst into fits of laughter. If the truth be told, The Mad Major was lucky he wasn't lumbered with the nickname 'Hop-along' right there and then.

There was another prisoner who fell victim to Doctor Manson's rather abrupt manner. Or perhaps, in this case, it would be more accurate to say Doctor Manson's manner fell victim to the nutcase, Alec Fisher, otherwise known as **Fish**. It so happened that Fish had a rather strangely shaped, bridgeless nose. It started between his eyes all right but, instead of angling forward and outward, the bridge of his nose was distinctly concave, only the very tip venturing to poke itself out into the world. Viewed from the side there was no denying Fish's snib strongly resembled a miniature ski jump. However, although the inverted shape of his nose had not appeared to trouble Fish thus far in his life, it suddenly it became an obsession of his to have it reshaped to a more acceptable appearance. As a medical matter, this desire necessitated a visit to Doctor Manson's morning surgery.

'Breath in through your nose,' Doctor Manson instructed Fish upon hearing his request.

Fish obliged, successfully snorting a full lungful of air into his body via his snout.

'There's nothing wrong with your nose, Fisher. Get out and stop wasting my time.'

'But I want it fixed,' Fish told him. 'I want it to look normal.'

'Out!' barked the doctor. 'There's nothing wrong with you.'

A week later, Fish once again stood in front of the good doctor. The same request was followed by same denial. 'Out!' said Manson, affording him only one word this time.

A couple of weeks later, an undeterred Fish marched back into the surgery once again. 'It's my nose,' he said. 'I want it fixed.'

'I've told you already, Fisher,' said a weary Doctor Manson, trying to reason with him, 'I cannot do anything for you. There is nothing wrong with your nose.'

At this Fish pulled a large PP9 battery from his pocket and swung it hard against the bridge of his hooter three times, spraying the office desk with blood and snot.

'Well, there fucking is now!' he told an astonished Doctor Manson.

Fish's ploy worked too. A few months later, he was walking about with his nose covered in bandages which when removed exposed a perfectly shaped proboscis.

Fish was, of course, mentally subnormal. In my opinion, he should have been certified at his trial and locked up in Carstairs, Scotland's institution for the criminally insane. He was actually serving life for the murder of an old woman. No one knows the reason for his offence and he was incapable of giving any explanation himself but the facts are these. Fish murdered this woman and left her dead in the backyard of some tenement houses. Needless to say, when her body was discovered, there was a terrible furore but no one knew anything about her death. The police made numerous appeals for information, hundreds of people were interviewed and some arrests were even made but nobody spoke to Fish.

Several weeks later, a coalman was returning to his lorry when he spotted a man scuttling up a common close with a stolen bag of coal on his back. The coalman gave chase but, when he reached the close, the man was nowhere to be seen. A policeman happened to be passing at the time and the angry coalman explained the situation to him, reasoning that, as the thief had disappeared so quickly, he must have taken refuge in one of the flats or possibly might even live up the close. As a result of this train of thought and anxious to clear up the crime, the policeman began knocking on doors and, in doing so, he cleared up a much bigger crime than he ever imagined.

After three or four negative responses, the copper rapped on the door of Fish's flat and was just about to enquire about the missing coal when the occupant spoke out in a most disparaging tone of voice. 'Call yourself polis?' Fish derided the constable. 'Three weeks since I done her and you're just coming for me now!'

Fish was arrested, later pleading guilty to the woman's murder at the High Court where he was sentenced to life imprisonment.

Well, there you are – I did say he was mentally subnormal.

Mind you, it would be safe to say that a high percentage of the cons in Peterhead were sadly lacking in the mental-agility department. The next anecdote illustrates a typical example of the mentally challenged.

21

HAMMY TAKES THE BLAME

Hammy was a member of the Paisley branch of one of the Loyalist organisations in Northern Ireland. Altogether there were about six members of his faction doing time in PH, all of them having been found guilty of being in possession of firearms and attempting to smuggle them into Ireland, allegedly to further the cause of their fellow members.

It was true that they did have guns – or, more accurately, bits and pieces of guns – but the fact is they did not have one *complete* gun and none of the so-called weapons they did possess was actually in working order. Nevertheless, when they attempted to board the ferry to Northern Ireland at Stranraer, Special Branch officers swooped and the entire 'unit' was arrested and taken to the nearest police station for interrogation.

Once in the police station, the gang was lined up and an officer of the Special Branch approached them and walked up and down the line for a couple of minutes before addressing himself to one, Bob Murray. 'So this is your little gang, Murray, is it?'

Of course Bob wasn't too happy about being dug out as the leader of the group, knowing that this put him in the limelight and thus would attract more of the judge's attention when it came to sending him down.

But his worries were short-lived. A loud, authoritative voice sounded out, 'Hold it!' James Hamilton stepped forward. 'Hold it, right there. I'm the commanding officer of this unit. If you want to speak to anyone, you speak to me.' Well, it was a case of Hammy by name and Hammy by nature as the bold James stuck himself right in the doo-doo when the Special Branch officer accepted his admission and turned his attention on him.

It turned out that Hammy was indeed the commanding officer, having been promoted to the rank of major for the simple reason that he was the only member of the unit who held a driving licence and he was the owner of a clapped-out old van – the very van in which the aforementioned 'weapons' had been found. With Hammy's admission of leadership and the fact that the 'weapons' had been found in his van, the Special Branch officer had more or less all the evidence he needed to get the gang remanded in custody, allowing the authorities time to make a deeper investigation into the functions of the unmasked Loyalist unit.

The 'facts' that were uncovered during the trial certainly made for lurid reports in the tabloid press with headlines like: 'TORTURE GANG UNMASKED'; 'KIDNAPPED AND KNEECAPPED'; 'ELECTRIC DRILL TORTURE' etc. etc. These evocative words definitely made eye-grabbing headlines and certainly sold newspapers to a public desperate to devour the daily 'exclusives' and insider 'exposés' on the actions of the torture gang that, according to official claims, terrorised the people of Paisley.

However, the truth behind the tales of torture and mayhem allegedly unleashed upon the innocent public was much more prosaic than the accusatory headlines peddled by members of the fourth estate, of whose working practices it has been already been said, 'Never let truth get in the way of a good story'. This maxim was certainly applied in full by the scribes who reported on the 'Paisley Torture Gang' trial. Reading the reports, one would imagine that the Loyalists of Paisley were grabbing people off the streets, taking them down to a dingy cellar, strapping them to a chair and torturing them to within an inch of their lives. Electric drills and pickaxe shafts, according to reports, were only some of the instruments used on anyone who became a target and was unfortunate enough to fall into the hands of this 'terrorist' gang. What a load of bollocks!

I was in PH along with most of the members of the Paisley Loyalist squad and, when the time came, I was roped in to help some of them prepare their submissions to the parole board. I can clearly remember reading the reports and statements from the trial and being struck by how different the facts were to the wild reports that had appeared in the press.

It turned out that, far from grabbing and torturing innocent members of the public, the only persons to come under any disciplinary proceedings by the unit were, in fact, all active members of that very unit. The persons that had been 'tortured' were all members who had committed 'offences' such as missing a meeting of the unit, being overdue with their membership subscriptions or exhibiting a lack of effort by failing to sell a satisfactory number of Loyalist magazines or newspapers at Ibrox. It was simply a case of the leaders feeling that, as a paramilitary force, they must have rules and there had to be penalties for breaches of these rules. Hence it was only members of their own unit who could break the rules and come under the jurisdiction of their courts martial and punishment pantomime. Irrespective of what had been reported, that's what it was – a pantomime.

What would happen was that the miscreant, if judged guilty, would be blindfolded before being taken into the basement and tied to a chair. Of course, this would constitute torture in itself if it was all really serious but the fact is that these adjudications and punishment sessions were a weekly occurrence carried out in front of all the unit members and everyone knew exactly what was going to happen. Tied to the chair the 'victim' would have his trouser leg rolled up to above the knee. A Black & Decker drill would be plugged in and given a few buzzes to make sure the target knew it was switched on and ready for action.

The 'charges' would then be read out to the member tied to the chair and the punishment – being drilled in the kneecap – would be announced. Once again, the drill would be sounded at the ear of the prisoner and everything would seem ready to proceed. The unit's administrator of justice was known as **Snoopy** and he would then kneel down in front of the guy in the chair and make the drill spin again before touching the guy on the knee with the end of a ballpoint pen or a pencil. The 'victim' would then get a final warning along the lines of, 'Well, I'll let it go this time but if you commit one more offence you really will get kneecapped.'

The entire thing was a charade and everyone present knew it. They witnessed the same thing every other week and, so far, no one had ever actually been physically hurt. I dare say the guy in the chair would feel a little apprehensive in case he became the first but, deep down, they would know that nothing was actually going to happen to them. As a matter of fact, the only injury suffered during one of these so-called torture sessions was the time when someone distracted Bob Murray's attention as he was buzzing an electric drill close to the guy's ear and, when he turned, he moved the drill bit, tangling the guy's forelock in it and pulling the hair out by the roots.

I can clearly remember writing on Bob's parole submission that not one single person ever required so much as an Elastoplast for any injury caused by his 'torture'. I like to think that, by pointing this out to the parole board, I influenced their decision in Bob's favour and I was happy to see him released early on parole.

In another place and at another time, the case would have been laughed out of court but the Special Branch needed a trial to show they were doing their job and made a mountain out of a molehill to produce a victory for their department.

At the end of their trial at the High Court, Hammy, as the self-confessed leader of the unit, was sent down for eighteen years while Bob Murray, Snoopy and the rest of the group received sentences of up to twelve years.

It was when I was talking to Snoopy in the tailors' shop a couple of years later that I mentioned to him that, if I had been in his outfit, I would have outranked them all.

'How's that?' he asked and I remember him looking at me in surprise.

'Well, I happen to have a pilot's licence,' I reminded him (this fact had been reported by the press at the time of my trial), 'and, if Hammy got made a major because he held a driving licence, surely someone with my qualifications would be promoted to a general at the very least?'

22

WATTY VERSUS ANDY BUNNET AND A FEW PETITIONS

A Hall was reserved for prisoners who were considered more dangerous and most of its inmates would be serving sentences running into double figures. As well as these long-term prisoners, it always housed around twenty or so guys doing life sentences and even one or two double lifers to go along with them. The trouble with lifers was that they were a cynical lot and they operated a policy of causing lots of trouble for the first five or six years of their sentences and made a point of giving the screws and even some of the cons plenty of aggravation. They would cause all sorts of trouble and I mean serious trouble like fighting, smashing things up, refusing to work, sabotage, throwing the food from the hotplate all over the place and doing anything else to disrupt the system. Typically, they'd carry on doing this for the first few years of their time.

However, as they passed into the fifth or sixth year of their sentences, they would gradually let themselves be seen to change for the better. They would stop being involved in subversive activities, taking no part in the endemic fighting and prison-wrecking. Their behaviour at work would improve and there would also be a noticeable change in their manner towards the screws. Cells would be cleaned up and kept neat and tidy and family photos put on display. The final step in this 'transformation' would see them going to Bible class and regularly attending church services.

Naturally the governors, prison psychiatrists and screws took all the credit for this 'improved behaviour', claiming that it was their 'treatment' that had rehabilitated the prisoner. 'See, our system works!' they would cry. 'Look at the change in this man.' And as a reward, our canny man would find himself upgraded to the 'privilege hall' where he could start thinking of liberation in three or four years' time. As I said, it was all dead cynical. But, believe me, it did work. A lifer could get out years earlier if he could adopt and stick to this long-term ploy.

I realise I've digressed there but I thought it might interest the reader to learn something of the guile and wile of doing long-term time. However, now it's back to the realities of life in the cell blocks and the crackpot, **Andy Bunnet**.

Extra searches were all part and parcel of being an A-category prisoner and we could expect snap searches at any time. Most of the screws kept things at a reasonable level of a daily cell search and, once a week, a strip-search. After all, we were searched twice every day on returning from work and, apart from pieces of cloth and home-made denims cobbled together from prison overalls, there was little opportunity to build up a tool kit or arsenal. But there was one screw, Andy Bunnet, who took his job more seriously than all the others put together.

Aye, Andy Bunnet – it's a name to conjure with but you would need the penmanship of Charles Dickens to be able to describe him with any degree of illumination. He was an introverted, taciturn, gaunt-faced, narrow-minded, Wee Free (a member of a strict, God-fearing religious sect based in northern Scotland) who was also a megalomaniac, a zealot and a dullard – as well as being an all-round fucking nutcase. All of these qualities could be applied to Andy Bunnet in equal measure.

Of course, calling anyone 'Bunnet' would automatically clue any Scotsman up the fact that, to earn such a nickname, there had to be something odd about the particular person's headgear. In Andy Bunnet's case, this is perfectly true and, if you were to line up fifty uniformed screws from Peterhead and asked any stranger to ID the person they thought might be called Andy Bunnet, no one would have the slightest problem in digging out the aforesaid party. It follows then that there must be something about this article of clothing that draws the eye or, in Andy Bunnet's case, stops the eye dead!

In a way, you might say that The Bunnet, as his nickname was often abbreviated to, was fortunate in having a huge pair of ears that acted as ledges to prevent his uniform cap falling halfway down his face, while his long wedge of a nose prevented the peak tilting forward to almost obscure his visage completely. How he ever got a start in a uniformed job remains one of the mysteries of the Scottish Prison Service. (I dare say that even the most inattentive reader will by now suspect a slight prejudice on my part regarding my opinion of Andy Bunnet.)

Notwithstanding all of the above-mentioned defects – or perhaps it was because of them – Andy Bunnet was appointed the full-time library officer. The job was actually a sinecure as all The Bunnet had to do was sit hidden away in his little office behind the sick bay, issuing the odd magazine or newspaper that had been posted in to an inmate. The fact that he was hidden away was, I suspect, the real reason behind his appointment. His actual knowledge of books was so negligible and he was himself so inarticulate that, when it was necessary for the prison 'librarian' to visit the Aberdeen main library, the governor had to ask one of the civilian educational tutors to accompany him to do the talking.

Although he was no doubt happy 'working' away in the library, there was always one aspect of a prison officer's job that The Bunnet was loath to forego – strip-searching the 'connies', as he referred to the inmates, and turning over their cells. He revelled in this occupation, his vocation in life being to deprive any prisoner of any article or item that was not specifically allowed. Extra magazines or books were pounced upon, their origins demanded and, regardless of explanation, they were impounded anyway. If there were any items in your cell that had not been officially permitted, they would be gleefully confiscated and consigned to Andy Bunnet's plastic bag. Included in his haul were things like music tapes, records and even magazines borrowed from a pal – if they weren't on your card and listed as 'in use', off they went. No excuses were permitted or listened to, your words of protest being overridden by the repetitive, highly censorious words 'Nay, nay, nay!' which were accompanied by a righteous non-stop shaking of The Bunnet's head as another treasured acquisition disappeared into his bag.

It seemed that catching prisoners out was Andy Bunnet's sole mission in life and, on the odd occasion when he did make a serious find, such as a blade or a tool of some kind, he would stand proudly at the door of the wing looking on as the unfortunate inmate was borne off to the cells. There was no doubt that Andy Bunnet was a zealot and a stickler for rules when it came to cell searches.

There was one occasion when a rumour went about that a prisoner, a well-known escape artist, had a key hidden away in his cell. Andy Bunnet became obsessed about the existence of this alleged key and took it upon himself either to find it or to lay the rumour to rest. One day – his day off, believe it or not – he appeared in overalls with a huge hammer in his hands, determined to settle the matter one way or another.

Bent on his mission, the Bunnet disappeared into the suspect's cell – a room no bigger that about seven foot by twelve foot that contained only the bare necessities of a bed, a table, a metal folding chair, one small cupboard and one hanging rail for a jacket and shirt. For hours, he could be heard rumbling about, banging and hammering behind the door in a fanatical search for the mythical key. Eventually, after hours of labour, he emerged from the cell, hammer in hand and white from head to foot, having literally chipped the very plaster from the walls. The bed had been broken, the bedding itself torn apart and tossed in a corner beside the remains of the small cupboard and the hanging rail that had been torn from the wall and destroyed. But, it has to be admitted, he emerged triumphant, brandishing a small piece of metal that either was a key or could be made into one. He strutted – well, as much as somebody with his puny physique could strut – out of the hall. The zealot was vindicated at last.

One of the big pastimes in Peterhead, for the football players anyway, was the daily lunchtime kick-about in the exercise yard. Now Andy Bunnet would always try and avoid crossing the yard when this game was on mainly because he always became the target for catcalls and other verbal insults. In the hurly-burly and shouting of the players, it was impossible for him to identify his denigrators so, to avoid any confrontation, he usually took the long way round.

However, one day he must have been in a hurry and ill advisedly cut across the yard, scurrying to cut his ordeal as short as possible. I don't know whether it was by luck or judgement but one of the men lobbed the ball into the air and, lo and behold, it struck Andy Bunnet's bunnet, knocking it right off his head and exposing a hitherto unsuspected bald dome of improbable dimensions. This unexpected exposure of The Bunnet's bald pate led to an immediate outburst of catcalls and insults being aimed at him. What a carry-on there was as Andy went ballistic, ramming his cap back on his head and yelling for the player to be put on report. But the other screws were laughing as loud as anyone else as voices were raised, advising The Bunnet to try hair restorer and recommending that he buy a wig.

Seeing there was nothing any of his colleagues were willing or able to do, Andy Bunnet scurried quickly away, anxious to escape the torrent of abuse that assaulted his ears. The episode became the joke of the day and one man even took things a bit further.

As I stated earlier, nobody liked Andy Bunnet – a state of affairs that generally did not seem to bother him one way or the other. In fact The Bunnet actually seemed to revel in the hatred and animosity he generated because at last, in a life full of mediocrity, he was getting noticed – even if it was by way of hatred and abuse. But there was one man who really got under The Bunnet's skin – the ubiquitous Walter Ellis, aka **Watty**. Without fail, Watty showed total disregard for and complete indifference towards The Bunnet, ignoring him as if he was the invisible man. For years, the two duelled as The Bunnet attempted to impose his will on Watty by abusing his authority. He was always trying to find something he could put Watty on report for and would make extra cell searches and constantly confiscate bits and pieces Watty used in his cell hobbies. However, not once did he elicit a response from the permanently poker-faced Watty. Finally, after years of trying to get a reaction, Andy Bunnet became so desperate that he offered Watty a job in the prison library.

A reaction at last! Watty raised his head and looked into Andy Bunnet's eyes for a few seconds before bursting into laughter. 'Work in the library!' he ejaculated. 'You, you fucking idiot! You torture me for years, put me on report, take my hobbies away, turn me over and wreck my cell and now you want me to work in the library with you? I wouldn't work with a clown like you if they offered to let me out tomorrow, you fucking half-wit!'

Well, back now to The Bunnet's baldy head.

You can always judge to within a day or two when you are due a heavy turnover rather than the quick daily spin that was part of a security prisoner's routine. So Watty was prepared when Andy Bunnet appeared at his door ready with his torch, stick and plastic bag. Working with his usual zeal, The Bunnet soon uncovered a package that Watty had apparently 'concealed' under his mattress. Rubbing his hands the Bunnet opened the package to reveal a plastic bag full of hair clippings along with numerous magazine and newspaper advertisements for wigs and hair-restoring concoctions. Along with these items was a note addressing the parcel to Andy. An apoplectic Bunnet promptly placed Watty on report for gross insolence and rushed him down to the cells.

The following morning, at the governor's adjudication in the orderly room, Watty calmly informed the governor that, as he was serving a sentence of twenty-one years, he fully expected to leave the prison bald-headed and was merely preparing the way by sending his friend, Andy, the cuttings of hair to see if he could make a wig from them. The adverts for hair-restorer were so that Andy could check up on the most efficacious treatment and so be in a position to advise him (Watty) on the best course to take for the restoration of his hair when he was eventually released.

The governor could barely restrain his grin as he 'carefully considered' Watty's defence before advising Andy Bunnet he was dismissing the case.

You will remember how in the last story Watty jeered at Andy Bunnet for being so presumptuous as to even consider the idea that he would work for him in the prison library. The following anecdote gives an example of why Watty had more than enough reason for his outburst.

The Bunnet was a narrow-minded teuchter and it seemed that his sole mission in life was to torment and irritate prisoners. No one got away with anything when he was on duty – The Bunnet saw to that – and you could expect him at your door at any time, ready to annoy you with a strip-search. Eventually Watty got so fed up with The Bunnet's constant strip-searches that he penned an official letter of complaint, a petition, which he sent to the Secretary of State for Scotland:

To the Right Honourable Secretary of State for Scotland

Dear Sir,

I would like to complain about the constant strip-searches I have to undergo here in Peterhead Prison. Most of the time they are pretty normal and do not give me any cause for concern. However, there is one particular turnkey [Watty insisted in calling all screws turnkeys] who is disturbing me with his zeal when carrying out these searches. At least once or twice a week this turnkey, Andy Bunnet, [Watty also refused to acknowledge proper names], insists on coming to my cell and giving me a strip-search. Now I realise that he is allowed to do this and I am not complaining about his seemingly insatiable desire to see me in the nude. But this Andy Bunnet always makes me strip down to my vest, then gets me to pirouette around my cell like a demented ballerina so he can freely inspect my bare buttocks and my other dangly bits.

It is obvious to me that Andy Bunnet is a pervert; I can tell by the way his eyes pop open and his breathing sounds funny when he is inspecting me. However, if he gets his kicks out of watching me spinning around in my vest with my private parts merrily jiggling up and down, that is entirely up to him. In fact I am not complaining about his perversion. What I am complaining about is that I am beginning to get to like it!

Yours faithfully

Walter Ellis

Petitions like this one were a constant source of amusement for us cons but of course not all of them were funny. Sometimes a con would have what he considered a real grievance and, on getting nowhere through the local complaints procedure, he would resort to writing a petition. However, 'last resort' would be a more appropriate description of the paper exercise of writing to the Secretary of State for Scotland. I mean to say, do you think for one minute that the Secretary of State ever clapped his eyes on a petition from a convict? Besides, it didn't matter what you wrote or who replied to it, the answer was invariably the same – 'Please inform the prisoner that, after careful consideration, the Secretary of State finds you have no grounds for complaint.'

Fast Eddie Andrews – a guy who, true to his nickname, was always rushing about – was another inveterate petition penner, who got so frustrated by the repetitive 'no grounds for complaint' reply that he decided to really put the process to the test. Grinning maniacally, he wrote a petition in utter gibberish, along the lines of:

> Dear Sir, Yjr kgpt yr dommy dllyp;y fisyylh dkdky rldsylyy iy y nn syss snf yi ld I hr. Orkerdr git ybr ttrkrsdr ig ygud ns bud rtrb frnsbfrf unnrfusyrkt. Pkrsdr br ibkuhrf yi vskjyy iyy ny ubdytvyuibd giteuth. Uv yiy ci bixklg fdokt gxy ghd dnc ov ghd cxmongh ghdn ig sill zll d yiuyr iwb faykt abd U cab di bi nire.
>
> Yours sincerely,
>
> E. Andrews

'There,' Eddie said, triumphantly waving his latest petition in front of his admiring pals before despatching it on its way, 'this will really fuck their minds up.'

Six impatient weeks later, Fast Eddie was delighted to be called up in front of the governor to receive his reply.

'Name number and sentence to the governor and say "Sir"!' The usual orders were barked out as Fast Eddie, grinning all over his face, marched into the orderly room.

The governor opened the envelope and prepared to read out the 'carefully considered' reply. He studied it for a few moments, slowly shaking his head, before finally passing it to the waiting Eddie.

'Here, Andrews,' he said, 'you'd better read this for yourself.'

Fast Eddie stared at the paper for several seconds before bellowing out, 'Whit the fuck's this? Ah cannae read this shite!'

The governor took the paper back and looked at the writing again. It went something like this:

Okeadt ubgtin yhr ptidonrt sdter vsreful vondifrtsyion yhr
Drvtrvstt ig Dysr ginff uou hsd no htounfd gto vompjut.
Yours faithfully, Secretary of State

'Well, it's quite plain to me, Andrews,' the governor told the puzzled prisoner. 'The answer quite clearly states: "Please inform the prisoner that, after careful consideration, the Secretary of State finds you have no grounds for complaint".'

'About turn, quick march! Next!'

Fast Eddie's baffled expression told its own tale to the waiting prisoners – fucked again!

The moral here was clear – you will never beat the system.

Howard Watson, an ex-policeman serving life for double murder and one of the better-educated men in Peterhead, once wrote a petition complaining about the food:

Dear Sir,

I wish to complain about the constant serving of cabbage as the vegetable portion of my lunch. Every day for months now there has been no variation in this part of my diet and I feel I am beginning to turn into a cabbage myself. Now I do realise that a change is expected of us whilst in prison. What I did not realise was that you would try to make this metamorphosis occur from the inside out and I am finding this, quite literally, rather a tasteless struggle. I really would appreciate it if you could see your way to providing an occasional change of vegetable with my lunch.

Yours etc.

Needless to say, the answer he got lived up to all our expectations – 'Please inform the prisoner etc. etc. etc.'

23

CHRISTMAS CELEBRATIONS

Christmas in Peterhead was certainly nothing to write home about – no Santa Claus ever made an appearance there – but we did get two days off work and £1 each from the Common Good Fund (which we had all paid into ourselves anyway, by way of a weekly pay deduction) as well a couple of good meals that proved Tom Soya could cook if he really wanted to. On top of that there were always one or two cons you could count on to make that extra effort to mark the occasion.

There was Joe Meechan, known as **Joe The Meek**, a long-term resident who always organised a couple of bingo sessions over the holiday – you paid a twist of snout or a couple of roll-ups per card. And there was always a clutch of guitar players and a couple of singers only too pleased to set up a concert of sorts for a literally captive audience.

So festive seasons weren't up to much and that's a fact. But tensions lessened as tacit truces were temporarily observed and you could definitely feel an air of celebration over the Christmas holiday. As well as this, we were all very aware that the start of a New Year was just one week away and that certainly heightened the general feeling of well-being.

The final week of the year always seems to drag but then suddenly it would be midnight on the thirty-first – Hogmanay! There's one silent beat, as if everyone is taking a breath, and then bedlam breaks loose and a huge volume of sound wells from the cells. The cons cheer and scream at the top of their voices and start banging their doors with metal dinner trays, steel soup bowls, chairs, the heels of their boots – anything that will raise a noise. Simultaneously, the foghorns of the Peterhead fishing fleet would blare out across the harbour, their cacophony adding to the madness inside. The New Year has arrived!

Maybe it's because the holidays interrupt our monotonous daily routine but it would always take a couple of weeks for us to settle back into the rut again and January is always considered a 'slow' month in prison. But for some lucky cons it is their final year and they go around on January the first with wide smiles on their faces, shaking hands and telling everyone they've 'cracked it'. It doesn't matter if their liberation date falls within days or right at the very end of December that year, they are now able to answer the perennial question of 'How long have you got to do?' with the smug reply, 'I'm out this year.'

Everyone enjoys a certain amount of satisfaction at the turn of the year. It's the one-down-another-to-go-syndrome sense of victory. Done it! Bring on another one! I can handle this! Everything is suddenly one year closer. Normally reticent guys will openly calculate dates when the preparation of parole papers should begin, discuss their chances of success and start planning what they'll do if parole is granted. The landings buzz with talk of time – counting time, handling time, doing time. Everyone is optimistic and some guys even talk about going home.

But the New Year euphoria would soon come to an abrupt end when we'd line up in the yard on a cold winter's dawn to be counted off and marched away on the first morning work parade of the year. It was guaranteed that some wag would sound out a long drawn-out, 'Hi, ho-o-o-o . . .' Another voice, in remarkable counterpoint, would echo, 'Hi, ho-o-o-o . . .' Then the entire work parade would sing out the rest of the words, 'Hi, ho, hi, ho, it's off to work we go!' Reality is reborn. We're in Peterhead and no one's going anywhere but down the Burma Road.

24

COODGIED

I know I said that I was not going to go on about the gangs of Peterhead but there is one gang that I cannot fail to mention and, believe me, at least half the prisoners in PH were fully paid-up members. What's more, the tentacles of this particular gang spread insidiously across the entire prison estate both in this country and, with obvious linguistic differences, abroad. In the UK, they are known as the **Coodgie Gang** and many a hardened con has been spotted ducking furtively aside to avoid the approach of a known member.

Attributes for admission to the gang are simple – with an eagle eye, well-honed stalking skills and the ability to make a perfectly timed swoop on an unsuspecting mark being basic requirements. If you have these, along with a brass neck and an ingratiating smile, topped off by a whining, 'poor-me' voice, you have all the necessary attributes for membership of the Coodgie Gang.

You might think you are alone and unobserved as you sneak your snout tin out to grab a fly smoke but it is a known fact that at least one member of the Coodgie Gang will mysteriously materialise by your side and you will hear the dreaded words: 'Coodgie [could you] gie's a wee puff o' that, pal?' It's like getting Tangoed. You're caught red-handed with the snout in your hands and the smile of the Coodgie man is there in your face like a *Big Issue* seller. For him it's a fait accompli, for you it's a roll-up and you've been Coodgied again.

Every demand is always delivered in an appropriately obsequious tone and manner, the word 'Coodgie' prefixing any request: 'Coodgie gie's a skin [fag paper]?'; 'Coodgie gie's a biscuit?'; 'Coodgie gie's a magazine?'; 'Coodgie gie's some sugar, milk, tea, coffee etc. etc. etc.?' Whatever you possess, a Coodgie man desires.

One member of the Coogie Gang, **Tam The Tapper** Larkin, a man well known for his scrounging proclivities, had no shame about it either. In fact, Tam thought it was an admirable accomplishment to be able to scrounge his way through his time. And I am forced to admit that I was a victim to his constant tapping myself. I know it would have been easy to say no but I have my own little set of standards I work to and one of them is that I don't mind sharing things like sugar and tea bags and such like. I don't smoke and always had enough cash to buy things like that from the canteen. So, if someone asks for a spot of sugar and I have some in my cell, I will not refuse them – even if they do, like Tam The Tapper, take advantage and come every day.

Tam must have been coming to me for months – so much so that it simply became another part of the daily routine. Every day, just before lock-up, Tam's outstretched cup-carrying hand would appear through my doorway, followed by his head and shoulders bearing the most ingratiating grimace I have ever seen.

'Aye, Tam?' I would say, greeting him as if it had never happened before.

'Aye, Bing,' he would reply, his face almost ingratiating itself to death. 'Coodgie spare me a wee drop of sugar?'

'Aye, help yourself, Tam.' I gave him free rein with my sugar and, to be fair, he only ever took enough for the one cup (I hope!). Now I honestly didn't mind giving Tam some sugar every day – in fact, I found the daily pantomime amusing. Still, I found myself wishing that Tam would turn up and I could honestly tell him that I didn't have any sugar. Then one day it happened. I forget why I had no sugar that particular time – maybe I'd had more guests in than usual that week and my sugar had just run out a bit earlier than it normally did. Whatever the cause, I had no sugar and I couldn't wait for Tam to appear so that I could tell him so. Sure enough, dead on time, Tam appeared at my door.

'Aye, Bing,' he said. 'Coodgie spare me a wee drop o' sugar?'

'Sorry, Tam,' I replied, trying to keep the delight out of my voice, 'there's none left.'

'None left!' The bold Tam's voice expressed disappointment and there was a brief flash of confusion in his eyes. 'Aw, fuck it!' he finally said. Then, without even a blush, he looked me in the eye and asked, 'Coodgie just gie's a wee tea bag instead then?'

I could only shake my head. Coodgied again! I had to admit it – the guy was a fucking genius. Mind you, I always wondered what the daily tea bag donor thought when Tam appeared at his door that day with a request for a wee spot o' sugar. No doubt about it, Tam The Tapper was an unashamed Coodgie man to the core.

Despite Tam's daily request for sugar, tobacco was always the leading Coodgie request but phone cards are catching up fast. 'Coodgie spare a couple of units?' is becoming common parlance on the wings nowadays. Mind you, although they were a nuisance, there is no doubt that the Coodgie Gang added a certain colour to life in drab Peterhead. Their insidious presence forced you to learn new skills in avoidance techniques and diversionary tactics.

The struggle to repel their advances without causing offence was almost like living outside. The 'two-tobacco-tins' ploy came into being because of the Coodgies. An empty tin would be produced as evidence of poverty while your real tin remained out of sight in your pocket. It was the same with phonecards – a wise man showing an almost-used card to fend off any would-be tappers. You learned to keep items like tea bags, coffee, sugar, milk and biscuits hidden away in a cupboard, only to be taken out once your door was safely closed to acquisitive eyes. Another tactic was to anticipate an approaching Coodgie and get your own request in first. Then, when you were recognised as a fellow Coodgie, the rest would leave you alone and you might get a bit of peace. The only trouble with that particular move was that you could gain an unwanted reputation yourself but it was all part and parcel of surviving in jail.

25

GENTLE JOHNNY RAMENSKY – A LEGEND

I honestly feel that anyone writing any sort of book about Peterhead and its inmates must include the legendary safe-cracker, **Gentle Johnny** Ramensky. I realise that this chapter is more factual than humorous but I make no apology for that. Johnny was a war hero and should be remembered for that at the very least. His nickname, Gentle Johnny, derives from the fact that he was averse to any form of violence and always came quietly when apprehended by the police.

Of all the cracksmen that came out of Scotland, there is no doubt that Johnny Ramensky stands head and shoulders above his closest contemporaries. Born in Glenboig, Lanarkshire in 1905 of Lithuanian parents, Johnny had an austere childhood, his mother being left to bring up the family on her own when her husband was killed in a mining accident.

Leaving school at fourteen, Johnny followed in his father's footsteps and went down the mines. However, by the time he reached the age of sixteen, many of the mines were starting to lay off their men and Johnny joined the ranks of the unemployed. Unable to stand the cards-and-dominoes life of the passive unemployed, Johnny decided that his experience as an apprentice shot-blaster would stand him in good stead as a safe-blower and that is what he became. His safe-blowing career began in the early twenties when Johnny specialised in blowing safes in garages and small factories.

Eventually he was captured on the roof of a factory carrying his safe-cracking kit and sentenced to a term in borstal. From then on, through most of his twenties, he was in and out of prison. In 1934 he escaped from Peterhead Prison but was captured crossing the road bridge at Ellon where the police routinely set up a roadblock whenever an escape occurred. Taken back to Peterhead, he was promptly thrown into the punishment block where he was shackled hand and foot. News of this treatment caused a public outcry and forced the authorities to abandon the barbaric practice, leaving Johnny with the doubtful honour of being the last man to be shackled in Scotland.

In 1939, Johnny was sentenced to five years in Peterhead and he was approached by a War Office official in 1942, two months before his sentence was due to finish. All sentences in those days automatically attracted one third remission – currently, those serving sentences of up to four years are eligible for a remission of half their time while those doing over four years get a third. Johnny was taken to London where he was asked by the War Department to work behind enemy lines. Johnny agreed to this but had to return to Peterhead to complete his sentence before he could take up this work.

After his release from prison, Johnny was given a specialist course of commando training. He was also taught all about the latest explosives and allowed to practise on new safes. Once he had completed his training, Johnny was parachuted behind enemy lines to blow safes and steal military plans and he successfully carried out many missions for the British Army. During the invasion of Italy, Johnny blew open fourteen safes in one day in the headquarters of the German Army. But perhaps his greatest coup was blowing open Hermann Goering's safe in his house at Karinhall.

One story goes that Johnny was awarded the DCM (Distinguished Conduct Medal) another claimed that it was the MM (Military Medal). Whatever it was, if there was any medal awarded, Johnny Ramensky certainly deserved one!

Once he was demobbed, Johnny found it difficult to adjust to normal life and once again took up his criminal ways. He was caught in the act of blowing a safe in the north of England and because of his army record a 'lenient' five-year sentence was imposed.

In 1952, Johnny escaped from Peterhead again. His escape became big news, with sympathetic newspaper reporting now building him into something of a folk hero. But, once again, Johnny was recaptured at the same bridge at Ellon – and by the same police officer too! On his return to Peterhead, Johnny was swamped by letters from well-wishers.

After his release in 1955, Johnny decided to turn his hand to some literary effort but fell foul of the Official Secrets Act which forbade him to expose anything of his military career. Thwarted in his literary ambition, Johnny reverted to his 'tools' again. In the summer of 1955, he blew open the strongroom and two safes inside a bank, where he stole £8000 and the contents of several strongboxes.

In late 1955, Johnny was captured raiding a bank in Rutherglen, near Glasgow, and a severe judge, Lord Carmont (the man who smashed the Glasgow razor gangs in the fifties by handing out double figure sentences), sentenced him to a harsh ten-year term. Once again Peterhead was host to its famous prisoner.

While he was serving this sentence, another well-known Glasgow figure, **Darky Davidson**, who worked in the sick bay of the jail, helped Johnny with an escape plan. Using his privileged position, Darky lifted floorboards in the doctor's office and hid Johnny in the space underneath. The idea was for Johnny to stay hidden until the roadblocks were lifted and he could then get clear. Darky kept Johnny supplied with food and drink but impatience got the better of Johnny and he went too soon. His face was so well known that passengers on a bus spotted him walking along the road and reported the sighting to the police. Within hours, Johnny was once again recaptured and returned to Peterhead. His status as a folk hero rose to such a high that two folk songs were penned in his honour – 'Set Ramensky Free' was recorded and sung by the Scottish folk singer Roddy McMillan, while even Norman Buchan, a Member of Parliament, got into the spirit of things with 'The Ballad of Johnny Ramensky'.

Released from prison in 1964, it wasn't long before Johnny was once again facing a High Court judge, this time for being caught on the roof of Woolworth's store in Paisley. This time, a sympathetic judge let him off with two years. Then, in 1967, Johnny tackled another bank in Rutherglen but, by this time, the safes were getting better and Johnny's skills were on the wane. He packed so much gelignite into the space behind the keyhole that the blast blew out windows nearby.

The safe proved to be empty and Johnny was captured as he tried to flee the scene. Outside in the street, he was brought to the ground by a young constable who started punching Johnny about the head. In self-defence, Johnny struck out at the policeman and, as a result, was charged with police assault. Johnny pled guilty to the safe-blowing but indignantly defended himself on the assault charge. Known to everyone as 'Gentle Johnny', he was more upset about being charged with assault than the safe-blowing offence. Johnny was delighted when the jury returned a not guilty verdict on the assault charge and happily accepted a four stretch for the safe-blowing. The irony was that, although the safe had been empty, there was, in fact, a sum of £80,000 in an unlocked drawer that Johnny had missed.

As he grew older, Johnny found his acrobatic feats of climbing more and more difficult to accomplish and, in 1970, he fell from a roof and spent fourteen weeks in hospital. When he left the hospital, it was to begin a two-year sentence for this latest attempt.

Upon his release from prison after serving the two years, Johnny was once again caught on a roof at midnight but, as he had not actually broken into the premises, he got away with a one-year sentence for attempted burglary. This last sentence proved too much for Johnny and he collapsed in Perth Prison. Taken to Perth hospital, he died within a few weeks.

Johnny Ramensky's funeral in the Gorbals was attended by hundreds of mourners, including **The Great Defender**, the famous criminal defence lawyer Joe Beltrami, who came to show his genuine respect for a very brave, if misguided, man.

26

RIOTS, RIOTERS AND FIRE

Riots came and riots went, hunger strikes were a regular occurrence and outright rebellion was never far away in Peterhead. One time, Big Brian Hosie, Frank Stein, Frank McPhee, Mad Hadgey, John O'Boy Steele and a few others fought a pitched battle in the yard with the screws and won. They climbed on to the roof of the reception and punishment block with captured riot gear – shields, helmets and long white batons – and, for the rest of the day, they marched about the rooftop chanting aloud like gleeful children, 'We won the war! We won the war!' Two or three days later, after a visit from a Scottish Office official, a truce was declared and the rioters agreed to come down from the roof by thirteen hundred hours. But, as it turned out, the rooftop ruffians were set to have one final fling.

At about 12.30, just half an hour before the agreed surrender time, smoke began belching out from the reception building after the rioters broke in to the reception storeroom and set fire to the clothes and clothing records of the inmates that were kept there. Much to the frustration of those in authority, this was greeted with loud cheers from those cons lucky enough to see it from their cell windows. The fire brigade had been standing by but, although the flames were soon doused, nothing was saved. What hadn't been destroyed by fire was damaged by smoke and the hoses of the fire department had completed the destruction.

About three weeks after the fire, the insurance assessors arrived and every prisoner was interviewed regarding their loss. Naturally, with the clothing records having been destroyed, every con made the most of their claim. Guys that had been arrested in T-shirts, jeans and trainers were claiming for Chester Barrie suits, Ben Sherman shirts and Gucci shoes. Everyone, except the insurance company of course, had a field day. One guy even had the nerve to claim for a suitcase full of expensive clothing, plus the case as well. There was no argument – paid out in full! Word later filtered back that the insurance company considered the cons of Peterhead the best-dressed criminals in the UK!

A postscript to that particular story was that the screw in charge of prisoners' private cash (PPC) was run off his feet as the grateful cons spent their windfall on the newly permitted in cell possession of tape decks and record players. With each claim averaging around £200, there was a total of around £70,000 floating about. It was manna from heaven and made to be spent – and spend it they did.

For weeks afterwards, deliveries to the jail were made on a daily basis, every delivery requiring PPC cards to be altered and the cash signed off. Then the purchase had to be recorded, in triplicate of course, and sent down to reception to be signed onto the prisoner's property card. The lucky buyer was then marched down to the reception to sign for receipt of his purchase, sign it on to his property card then sign it out again as 'in use' – all typical prison bureaucratic rigmarole. With so much work being generated the screws should have been grateful to the fire-raisers for getting them lots of overtime. So, in a sense, you might say the fire benefited everybody in one way or another.

But, within a couple of months, the money was gone and things settled down again, leaving us with memories of the rebellion and laughing over the score from the insurance company.

If there was one thing you could count on from the cons of Peterhead, it was that they never did things by halves.

There have been rooftop riots in half the prisons in Britain, but not once did the authorities have to resort to the drastic measures it took to quell the convicts of Peterhead. Although there were several serious incidents during my time in Peterhead, I actually missed the main rooftop and hostage-taking riots by a few years. The really serious riots didn't take place until the mid eighties and early nineties, after I had left, and very serious some of them were too. On one memorable occasion in 1987, the cons rioted and took to the roof of A Hall with a hostage – a screw they called **Hess**.

This Germanic nickname perhaps throws some light on his character and why he was the chosen hostage. However, his real name was Jackie Stewart and there was no doubt that he was in very grave danger. In fact, the government viewed the situation so seriously that, after six days, a detachment of SAS soldiers was secretly flown in to break up the riot and rescue him, in an operation that remained secret for more than twenty years! And, afterwards, Hess, a typical penny-pinching Aberdonian if ever there was one, demanded overtime for the duration of his ordeal. He even worked it out – he calculated it would be 144 hours, including some at double time – and demanded it on top of the thousands of pounds compensation he received. But, as I have often said, all that could be another story.

27

SLASHER GALLAGHER

But never mind the cons, even the governor was known to take things to extremes at times. Perhaps it was the ambience of the place, the underlying tension, the short tempers and routine violence in Peterhead that caused people to behave irrationally at times. I suppose there must be some sort of psychological explanation. I do know that the screws there got an extra environmental allowance because of the alleged contaminating effect of constant association with lowlife cons affecting their own moral standards and personal lives. And they might have a point there too because, if ever there was a case of cross-contamination of standards, Square Go Gallagher, the prison governor himself, epitomised it. You may remember me mentioning his name earlier, when he had the altercation with Walter Ellis regarding the murder of a taxi driver. Well, it's the same guy and this story, although it takes a bit of believing, explains how Square Go Gallagher came to be rechristened **Slasher Gallagher**.

One of the cons, Robert (Bob) Brockie, a lifer who had been down the cells for months on self-imposed protection, had been told that he was going back on the wing. Bob wasn't too happy about this proposed move because the guy he had the problem with was still there and the grievance had not been settled. Believe me, Bob was scared.

Being on protection, Bob was allowed to have his toiletries 'in use' and, in his desperation to avoid a confrontation with his nemesis, he melted the plastic handle of his toothbrush and fixed a razor blade into it, making a very handy little chib (blade). His plan was simple – carry out a desperate deed and his tenure and safety in the cells was assured.

He knew that the governor did his rounds of the cellblock every morning, going into each cell and barking out the pointless question, 'Any complaints?' Usually the door was slammed and he was gone before the con could even formulate a reply, never mind voice a complaint. But this day things were to be different and Bob was on his feet, psyched up and ready to go. I can imagine the scene almost as if I had been present myself. The door crashed open, slamming back on its hinges as Square Go stepped in, already mouthing his question. Bob leapt forward and lashed out with his makeshift chib, catching Square Go on the cheek just below his left eye. Then, paralysed with fear he just stood there, dropping the blade on the floor. The shocked governor and staff froze as if they were in a snapshot but then Square Go picked up the blade and grabbed Bob by the throat.

'Chib me, you wee bastard?' he yelled and drew the blade down Bob's face. Christ, what a turn-up!

Next, obviously still fired up, Square Go Gallagher strode into the adjacent B Hall of the prison and stood on the bottom flat with the blade still in his hand. He was yelling out at the closed doors, 'I've just chibbed that bastard Brockie! Any of you want to do anything about it, you know where to come!' A few seconds later, having recovered from their shock, his escort hustled him away.

All I can say is that Gallagher was very fortunate indeed with his retinue that day. Not one of them cracked and I've seen screws 'putting in a paper' – i.e. reporting one of their workmates – for minor breaches such as eating prison food (I think they got brownie points for grassing).

Fortunately for Bob, he had only succeeded in nicking Square Go's cheek and the wound required no more treatment than a small Elastoplast strip. This was probably one of the reasons that, with the co-operation of Bob himself and the loyalty of his staff, they were able to execute a successful cover-up. With no witnesses willing to 'put in a paper', and Bob prepared to make up some tale about self-inflicted wounds, a deal was struck. In return for keeping his mouth shut, Bob was offered an immediate transfer to the safety and cushy conditions of the Barlinnie Special Unit. Satisfied beyond his wildest dreams, Bob agreed terms and the matter was settled.

The incident was the talk of the jail – if not the entire Prison Service. Even if the rumours and gossip did reach the ears of the Prison Service Head Office, they were simply just too bizarre to be believed. But no reports were ever filed and the incident apparently had never happened. With no defamation to his character, Square Go retained his good name, going on to peak out his career as the Director of Scottish Prisons. But the fact is that everyone in Peterhead knew the truth and, ever since that day in Bob's cell, Square Go Gallagher became known as Slasher Gallagher and, believe me, he was proud of it.

There is a postscript to this story too. Years later, when Slasher was the governor of Barlinnie Prison, the inmates rioted, wrecking one of the wings and climbing up on to the roof to protest against the brutal regime. The following morning a dramatic, front-page photograph appeared in a newspaper showing the demonstrating prisoners holding up a huge, bed-sheet banner bearing the words 'SLASHER MUST GO'. 'Christ!' the editor was said to have remarked. 'What sort of a guy is this Slasher character? What's he in for?'

'He isn't in for anything,' he was told. 'Slasher's the bloody governor!'

28

BIG WULLIE LEITCH –
THE SAUGHTON HARRIER

I have already mentioned Wullie Leitch's name in this book but I honestly think that a larger-than-life person such as Wullie deserves to have a chapter all to himself. Mind you, I always thought **Hans Christian** would have been a much more deserved nom de guerre for him than the one he was landed with because, if he could do nothing else, Big Wullie could certainly spin a spellbinding tale. Of course, once again, as with most con storytellers, the listener would be well advised to keep copious amounts of salt close to hand – especially when the porky pies start flowing from Wullie's well-exercised lips.

Harrier obviously implies that the so-named person had, at some time or another, been involved in the sport of running and this is indeed the case with Big Wullie Leitch.

Early in his career, Wullie had just begun a four-year sentence in Edinburgh's Saughton Prison for some criminal escapade and he wasn't too happy about it at all. However, being of sound mind and body, Wullie decided very early on in his sentence that prison was not for him. So, with his eye on rapid progress to a position of trust, he chose to become a model prisoner. As an ex-serviceman, I suppose the years of strict military discipline he had experienced in the Royal Navy helped Wullie to adapt to the rigorous regime that cons were put through during the early stages of their sentence in those tough old days.

As he appeared to have adjusted well to the prison routine, worked diligently at his mailbag sewing and willingly carried out any task asked of him, Wullie soon found himself moved on to the yard-cleaning party, where he was free to move around within the confines of the prison grounds picking up litter and generally keeping the yards and pathways looking spruce and tidy.

'You're a credit to the prison, Leitch!' was a compliment often paid to him by the governor as he passed by on his daily inspection rounds. Wullie, of course, would make a point of being seen to be working away most industriously whenever the entourage hove into sight.

However, despite his seemingly exemplary conduct, our Wullie, who was soon to be christened The Saughton Harrier, had only one thing on his very active and determined mind. He knew exactly what he was doing by doffing the cap and acting subservient to all and sundry. The muttered barbs of 'creep' and 'arselicker' from his fellow inmates rolled off his broad shoulders like water from a duck's back. He had a more important agenda and it would take more than a bit of name-calling to divert Wullie from his aim. By collecting brownie points day by day, he knew that he would soon be elevated to employment on the outside garden party, a target he had set his sights on from the first day he entered prison.

Wullie's strategy paid off when, after just six months of obsequiousness, he was handed the red armband of a trusted prisoner, along with a barrow, a shovel, a rake and various other garden implements with which to maintain the gardens that decorated the driveway of Saughton Jail. And, for a few weeks, he did just that. There was no doubt that, during his time on the job, Wullie made a great improvement to the driveway gardens – clipping here, digging there and trimming the ragged verges as well as neatly tidying up as he gradually moved along. But more importantly, as Wullie well knew, he was gradually gaining the trust of the watchful prison officers as he edged closer and closer to the garden area at the foot of the entrance drive and just out of sight of the main gate. Wullie timed his move to perfection, patiently holding back until the window, or morning rather, of opportunity he had been waiting for presented itself.

It was a sunny day in July 1967 and the local harriers club was holding an annual road race which, by a stroke of good fortune for Wullie, had been routed along Saughton Road right past the front of the prison. The screws had long since ceased even their cursory checks on the contents of Wullie's barrow – who would want to smuggle anything out of jail anyway? – and looked on uninterestedly as he trudged past them pushing his barrow through the gate and down towards the main road. Wullie worked away on the flowers for an hour or so, gradually edging his way round the corner and out of sight of the gate screws.

Wullie had timed things to perfection and was just tying the laces of his smuggled sandshoes (they call them plimsolls in England) as the first of the runners appeared, heading in the direction of Sighthill, a district Wullie knew well and a place where he had plenty of friends. Quickly stripping off his overalls to expose a suitably numbered prison PT vest and shorts, Wullie immediately metamorphosed from convicted criminal to hurrying harrier as he stepped forth and 'joined' the race, every inch the dedicated runner as he made his bid for freedom. And run he did because he wasn't seen again until months afterwards, when he was finally apprehended by the forces of law and order.

The novel manner of Wullie's disappearance made a good headline for the newspapers of the day, who promptly dubbed him the Saughton Harrier, a name that has stood the test of time. Mention the Saughton Harrier to any of the older cons in the system and they will nod their heads and smile, only too happy to recall the tale of Wullie's escape to freedom. So there you are – yet another example of how one little incident can generate a legend that is still talked and laughed about forty years after the event.

The Saughton Harrier, however, did not just win fame for his running-off-to-freedom escapade. He was also well known as an entertaining prison raconteur with a huge fund of tales from his kaleidoscopic past. Indeed, there are many tales of equal implausibility that I could relate but I think the following one illustrates the type of guy Wullie was – or aspired to be. Reading this most improbable tale of unintentional heroism should give the reader an insight into the unfulfilled Walter Mitty-ish dreams of Wullie Leitch, aka The Saughton Harrier.

By the way, I dare say most readers will think that I have given this story a very long title but then it was a very long story when originally related to me. In fact, it was so long that it livened up an entire morning that would otherwise have been just another boring day in Peterhead's tailors' workshop security party. I have actually reduced Wullie's tale to its bare essentials otherwise, with the wealth of irrelevant detail and wide ranging diversions indulged in by its original narrator, it would take up most of the notepaper I have to hand.

I ask the reader to sit back and enjoy this short tale in the tongue-in-cheek spirit in which it is offered.

Long since a fully paid-up member of the 'tall-tales gang', Wullie always began one of his entertaining stories with the innocent-sounding, 'Hey! Did I ever tell you about the time . . .?' Of course he hadn't but the trap had been sprung, the bait taken, the table set for him to relate yet another of his riveting revelations. I was quite pleased, therefore, one boring workday morning, to be addressed in the inquiring tone Wullie adopted when about to expose yet another facet of his vastly adventurous life.

'Hey, Bing!' Wullie called out to me one morning as I passed his worktable on my way back from the toilet.

'Aye, what is it, Wullie?'

He waved pudgy fingers at the chair opposite him and fixed me with 'that' expression on his face. Wullie possessed the knack of looking genuinely uncertain – his balding grey head would tilt to one side as his eyes would screw up in consideration, apparently not wanting to bore anyone with a repetitive tale. 'Did I ever tell you about the time I shot down an American jet plane in the South China Seas . . .' And here Wullie inserted a perfectly timed pause that any actor would have died for, as if his introductory words were of no special importance, merely a hook on which to dangle the real meat of the tale. He then added, 'With a sling?'

I worked hard at keeping a straight face as if his statement concerned nothing more exciting than another mundane, everyday occurrence. 'No, Wullie,' I had to admit, speaking calmly and hoping my eyes had not popped too wide. 'No,' I repeated, giving the impression that I had actually given the question some serious consideration. 'You've never mentioned it.' Then I made him happy. 'How did you manage to do that?'

'I never told you?' He screwed his face up, obviously annoyed at the omission.

'No,' I stated positively, 'you've never told me that before.'

'Ahh!' said Wullie as he settled into position, with his forearms resting on the table. His large, tired, slightly choleric face, with its pale, blue-grey eyes above a huge, purple veined, bulbous nose, leant heavily forward over his folded arms. 'Aye,' he said, after a pause that seemed to indicate he was getting his story right in his mind. '"The Man who Was Painting the Gun at the Back of the Boat" – that was a bit of a do, so it was. You see,' Wullie continued, his eyes staring earnestly into mine, 'it was when we were on an exercise in the South China Seas against the American Navy at the time. I was leading cook on the *Concord*, a frigate,' he informed me. 'Well, see when you're on these exercises? You have to hang about your battle station when you're no' at your real job – "At the ready" they call it – so you could get into position quick when the klaxon went off for action stations. Well, my battle station was the Bofors gun at the back of the boat and, as I told you, that's where I used to hang about in my ready position.' At this, Wullie gave an emphatic nod of his head. 'You see,' he said, 'you could never tell when that klaxon would go off. You could sit about all day and nothing would happen. Then, suddenly . . .' Wullie (also a born actor) looked startled. He jerked upright in his seat, put his clenched fist to his mouth, filled his cheeks with air and blew trumpet-like into his hand. '"Whooo! Whooo! Whooo!"' (Wullie always peppered his stories with action and realistic sound effects.) 'An' that was it! "Whooo! Whooo! Whooo!"' He underlined the urgency of the moment again. 'One minute you're sitting in the sun, next thing you're diving about like a madman, sticking on your helmet and climbing up intae your position.'

He made frantic climbing motions with his arms, his face registering the urgency of the situation as he thrust himself against the back of his chair, grasped imaginary gun controls and stared with narrowed eyes into danger-filled skies. So effective was his display that I had to make a conscious effort to stop myself looking apprehensively over my shoulder for the approaching enemy. Then, just as suddenly as his call to action stations had been, he subsided on to his elbows again. 'But most of the time you just hung about and waited.'

Wullie had a disconcerting habit of pausing during his stories and lapsing into long silences that made you wonder if he had forgotten what he was talking about. Then he would furtively cast his eyes round the surrounding area, throwing suspicious glances over his shoulders, first left, then right, as if he suspected someone of creeping up on him or perhaps eavesdropping on his conversation. The silence stretched on and on as Wullie continued to cast his eyes suspiciously about. Knowing how his mind sometimes wandered, I waited . . . and waited . . . and waited for him to resume his tale. Finally, thinking he had decided to eke out his story in instalments, I made a perfunctory rising movement.

'Hey!' he cried, fixing his mournful eyes on me. 'What's up? I'm no' finished yet.'

'Oh,' I grunted, settling myself back into my chair and looking expectantly at him.

'Aye,' he began again, casting his mind back over his story so far, 'but, when it wasn't action stations, you just hung about and waited and you can get a bit fed up just sitting on a boat deck. So I used to get myself a big tin of paint . . .' His hands exhibited a paint pot of generous proportions. 'And pass the time painting the gun. Well, one day I was getting ready to start painting the gun when I noticed the paint tin's lid hadn't been put on properly and a hard skin had formed on the surface of the paint inside so I had to lift this layer of skin off to get to the fresh paint underneath. You know how the skin goes dry and you can press your fingers into it and just, sort of, peel it off? Well, I picked off the skin and rolled it into a ball about . . .' he said, making a circle with thumb and forefinger, 'that size. They only use the best of paint on these boats, you know,' he informed me with a serious nod, before launching into the whys and wherefores of this special, super-duper, all weather boat paint – an aside I won't go into here because it took Wullie about half an hour to get his description of the paint across.

Eventually, after a final analysis of the paint's chemical composition, he got back to the main storyline again. 'Well,' he said, 'I had this ball of solid lead paint and was just going to chuck it overboard when I remembered my sling.' He nodded in emphasis. 'A good powerful rabbit sling it was too. You know the kind I mean – heavy square rubber attached to an aluminium frame. You can fire things for miles with them and this ball of lead paint made a smashing load for it – just the right size and weight.' He bounced an imaginary paintball up and down in the palm of his hand and nodded to himself again, failing to offer any reason for having such a strange weapon on board an ocean-going warship. 'Well, I had my sling in my hip pocket and I got it out – no kidding.' (Wullie often added 'no kidding' to his statements, doubtless believing it added a certain degree of veracity to his words.) 'I pulled the sling back as far as it would go.' He demonstrated his technique, stretching his left hand forward and slowly drawing back with his right hand which was firmly clutching his imaginary lead paintball as the invisible, taut rubber made his hand quiver with barely controlled energy and he screwed his eyes up in concentration.

'I got a right good pull at it.' Wullie spoke through teeth clenched with the strain of holding back the powerful weapon. 'The ball of paint felt really good . . . you know . . . tight, solid, ready to go.'

'"WHAP!"' The sound effect and sudden relaxation of his arm advertised the dispatch of Wullie's lead paint projectile. Then, with his tired old eyes becoming uncommonly keen, he followed the invisible trajectory of his imaginary missile. Suddenly his mouth fell open and I saw his eyes grow wide. A split second later, he ducked his balding head under the table and I flinched as some astonishing sound effects emanated from the vicinity of the floor.

'"Whooosh!" "Roarrr!" "Whanggg!" "Scooshhh!"' Onomatopoeia flowed from Wullie as he tried to vocalise a split second of sudden madness. You must, of course, realise that the art of storytelling, particularly in prison, is as much visual as oral and the way Wullie suddenly ducked his head and then slowly emerged from his shelter, with a haunted expression on his face as his hands described parabolic arcs, would have put a first-class mime artiste to shame.

I was pretty startled myself at the sudden turn of events and waited breathlessly for the rest of the story.

'What a fright I got!' Wullie admitted once he had re-established his position at the table.

I nodded, waiting . . . and waiting . . . and waiting . . . as Wullie engaged in yet another of his interminable silent interludes, casting suspicious eyes about, checking carefully over each shoulder, pursing his thick lips and nodding introspectively as his eyes focused on some distant memory. Either that, or he was 'creating' the rest of his tale. I waited, hoping for more, but, as the story seemed once again to have petered out, I started to rise hesitantly from my seat.

But this action immediately prompted Wullie back into speech. 'Aye. What a fright I got,' he repeated, nodding in confirmation of his earlier admission.

'What was it?' I ventured a question.

'A jet fighter plane,' Wullie replied, as if such a thing shouldn't be entirely unexpected. 'An American jet fighter plane,' he said, clarifying the nationality of the aircraft. 'The bandit had sneaked up on us and attacked the ship from the back. Next thing the tannoy goes . . .'

Making a megaphone with his hands, he very realistically relayed the message. '"All hands! All hands!" It was the captain speaking,' he informed me in a quick aside. '"All hands. This is the captain speaking. This is the captain speaking."'

I have to admit that Wullie's 'mechanical' voice sounded remarkably authentic.

'"We have just been struck by an air-to-sea missile and the ship is deemed sunk. Stand down action stations. Stand down action stations. We are returning to port."

'And believe me,' said Wullie as he leant across the table, his eyes as doleful as a beagle with mental problems, mentally commiserating with his ex-captain, 'he was really sick about it. I mean . . . It was only an exercise but he had lost his ship! If it had been the real thing, we'd all have been dead! And he was the captain. It would all have been his fault – a right black mark on his record. Oh, he wasn't pleased – the captain wasn't pleased at all.' Wullie mournfully shook his head.

'So what happened?' I asked, hoping to forestall another of his interminable silences.

'I'll tell you what happened,' (I hadn't doubted that for a moment) said Wullie, leaning halfway across the table, his jowls quivering with suppressed excitement. 'See when we got back to port in Korea and tied up at the dockside? A big black American motor pulls up alongside the ship and out stepped a spaceman!'

'A spaceman!' My outburst was totally involuntary.

'Aye. One o' these pilot guys,' Wullie confirmed. 'He was wearing a silver suit and a big white helmet and he stood there looking up at the boat while some other guys got out of the motor. And you should have seen them! One was an admiral and the other guy was a general.'

I stared at Wullie, willing him to continue.

'They came up the gangplank . . .' Wullie's fingers rose to his mouth. '"Phwee phweeee!"' His bosun's whistle reverberated round the workshop. 'And our captain went down to meet them. I couldn't see what was going on but next thing . . .' His fist flew to his mouth. '"Now hear this. Now hear this." It was the captain speaking,' he explained. '"Will the man who was painting the gun at the back of the boat report immediately to the bridge?" Well, that was it – I mean, they knew it was me. They only had to look at the duty roster.' His hand flew back to his mouth. '"Will the man who was painting the gun at the back of the boat report immediately to the bridge?" What could I do?' Wullie looked at me beseechingly.

I nodded sympathetically, sensing trouble in the offing.

'When I got to the bridge, they were all standing about and I went up to the captain and told him that I was the man who was painting the gun at the back of the boat. What else could I say?' Wullie looked mournfully at me and shrugged. 'I mean . . . I had to admit it. Then the captain says to me, "Wullie, what else were you doing besides painting the gun at the back of the boat?" Well, I thought to myself, I'm in trouble now all right. And I still had the sling in my pocket. "Come on, Wullie, what else were you doing?" the captain asked me again. No kidding, it was worse than a High Court cross-examination, so it was. There was no way out. I had to come clean,' he told me in a hopeless voice. 'So I pulled out my sling and told him I had fired a lump of paint with it.

'Next thing this pilot guy steps up to me and says, "So you're the guy who was painting the gun at the back of the boat?"'

At this, Wullie went into his silent routine again. I could have sworn he was hoping somebody – even one of the other cons – would step forward and admit that he had been the man who was painting the gun at the back of the boat. If he waited much longer, somebody would surely own up to it. I knew there was still more to come but Wullie was once again temporarily mute. I made as if to rise from my seat and successfully switched him on again.

'"Aye," says I,' Wullie burst into speech again. '"I'm the man who was painting the gun at the back of the boat." Next thing this pilot guy sticks out his hand and says, "Let me be the first to congratulate you, Buddy!" And he starts shaking my hand. Well, I didn't know what to do. He's standing there giving it big time with my mitt while the admiral and the general are watching us. Then the pilot told me . . .' Wullie leant forward and, in a nasal, transatlantic conspiratorial whisper, related the pilot's words, '"When I landed my plane back at the base, one of my ground crew noticed a streak of grey paint right under my cockpit and he asked how in the hell it had gotten there. 'Well, Buddy,' I told him, 'I remember seeing someone standing up and aiming something at me when I approached the back of the ship,' and I told him that it must have been the man who was painting the gun at the back of the boat. And he says, 'Well, Major, you've just been and done got yourself shot down. That was a direct hit on a vital part of the plane – so theoretically, sir, you're dead!'" Next thing my captain steps up and says to the pilot, "If you're dead that means that we were never sunk!"

'"You can bet on that!" the pilot says. "I was a dead duck before I launched that missile at you. Whatever the hell it was this guy fired at me, he hit me fair and square!".'

Wullie sat back in his chair. 'Well,' he said, 'that was that. We cast off and got back into the battle again. But see when we were at sea? The captain comes up to me and says, "Wullie, you're a hero. You saved the ship. Come on up to my cabin." And when we got to his cabin he opens a bottle of whisky – one of those big giant-sized bottles it was too – and he says to me that, any time I wanted a drink, I was just to come up to his cabin and help myself.'

'So that was you OK, then?' I observed. 'You saved the captain's ship and his reputation.'

'Oh, aye – nae bother!' Wullie was suddenly nonchalant, dismissing his heroic achievement with a shrug. 'Me and the captain were the best o' pals after that.' For a long moment he stared thoughtfully into space, no doubt considering what might have been. 'Aye,' he finally said, 'it was all a bit of a do, so it was.'

I waited for a few minutes as Wullie fell into a thoughtful, no doubt reminiscent, silence and he never noticed when I stood up and stole back to my machine, wondering whether or not he still had his faithful sling safely locked away in his property box in reception.

So there you are – the larger-than-life Wullie Leitch, The Saughton Harrier, is a man well worthy of a place in the history of Her Majesty's Prisons – as well as in the memoirs of a grateful captain of the Royal Navy.

Well done, Wullie!

29

SOME ODDBALLS AND
CARTOON CHARACTERS

Having a reputation as a bit of an intellectual, as well as the only con in the jail with a typewriter, I was always being asked to help other guys compose their letters, petitions or any other writing they were having difficulty with. I was not surprised, therefore, when one evening this con, a Moroccan milkman (I always get the exotics!) who lived in Edinburgh and was serving life for murdering his wife, came into my cell with a piece of paper in his hand, acting all secretive.

'Sshhh! Sshhh!' Abdul put his finger to his lips and looked furtively around, as if he suspected someone was following him. 'Is secret,' he whispered. 'Please, you don't tell anyone?'

'Come on, come on,' I said, impatiently holding out my hand for his note. 'Just give me the fucking letter and I'll type it out for you.' I didn't have time to muck about with all this secret-service stuff.

'Is secret,' he says again. 'You keep secret?'

'For fuck's sake, pal,' I told him, 'just give me the bloody letter.' I just wanted the job done and to get Abdul out of the way. 'C'mon – letter!'

'OK,' he said, 'you write for me, please.'

No messing about, I leant his note on my paper-prop and hammered it out. I'm a touch typist and never really pay all that much attention to what I'm typing; it's all just words to me. But this letter went along the lines of:

Dear Governor and Chaplain,

I am sorry. I kill my wife and now she is in heaven. I feel bad about this and I want to be with her again. I go to be with her now. No blame for you or anyone. I just want to be with my wife.

Abdul

What a load of shite, I said to myself, dashing it off and handing the finished letter back to him. 'There you go, Abdul. That do you?'

'Thank you. Thank you. You good man. I remember you in heaven.'

Aye, right, fucking idiot. I went back to my own work, totally dismissing the incident from my mind. Then, a few days later, around two in the morning, I was wakened from my sleep by noise and flashing blue lights outside my window. When I got up to look at the commotion, I saw an ambulance with paramedics unloading oxygen equipment from it.

Jesus Christ, I thought to myself, he's only gone and done it! Then a terrible thought struck me – the note! The bloody suicide note! And I'm the only con in the jail with a typewriter! 'Oh fuck!' I said aloud, with no thought for the demented Moroccan. 'They'll take my typewriter away.'

I listened at my door to the sounds in the hall – feet pounding upstairs, keys rattling and doors opening. Then a stretcher rushed past and the ambulance took off. I should never have written that note, I told myself. Now they'll take my typewriter away. At morning slop-out, I emerged from my cell waiting to be pounced on and hustled away to the cells. Then I spotted the Moroccan, large as life and emptying out his pisspot. What a relief! It wasn't him. My machine was safe.

It later transpired that one of the men in a two-man cell had assaulted his cell mate with a metal chair so severely that he had caused permanent brain damage. Prison black humour raised its head and the story went round that the injured guy had been reading one of my stories out loud and his cell mate hit him with the chair to shut him up. A pack of lies, of course! But I made up my mind about one thing – no more suicide notes for me!

I have mentioned before how a nickname can be earned and how appropriate it usually is. Lofty, Shorty, Banana Back and, of course, the highly descriptive Jelly Buttocks – they're all pretty much self-explanatory. But how does one manage to attract the appellation **Batman**? This becomes even more puzzling when you consider the puny physique of the owner of this colourful nom de guerre. Most certainly the tall stature and rippling muscles of the acrobatic, crime-fighting comic-book hero were not attributes enjoyed by our subject, John Higgins. Nor did he have sticky-out, bat-like ears that might have accounted for his unusual sobriquet. It, therefore, raises the question – just how exactly did John Higgins earn this name?

Let's start by saying that it all came down to the reason he ended up in prison, when, at his trial, it was disclosed that John had a certain propensity for dressing up in his comic-book hero's crime-fighting outfit. The difference between the two, however, was that John was more concerned with committing crime rather than following in his hero's footsteps. And, even more strangely, John had utilised the services of his attractive wife as a willing accomplice to his crimes.

John's and his wife, Margaret, lived near Byres Road and the University of Glasgow. Margaret was an attractive woman of about thirty, with dark Italian looks. The proud possessor of a well-curved, voluptuous body, she had no inhibitions about wearing skimpy clothing that allowed her to exhibit a cleavage as deep and interesting as the Grand Canyon. In short, for the red-blooded male students who populated the area, she was just the sort of slightly older woman who could jolt their hormones into supercharged overdrive. It was not surprising, therefore, that, whenever the fancy took her – or, more accurately, whenever the fancy took her husband – she would sally out to the student-rich hunting grounds of Byres Road, where she knew she would have no trouble attracting the lustful attention of any hormone-charged student she chose to bump into.

This was a diversion she regularly indulged in. In Byres Road, there are shops that display small ads offering rooms to let and her favourite place to approach young men was outside one of these shops. Her technique was simple and it was made all the easier because her chosen targets were already nibbling at the very same bait that she was about to offer. Having selected her quarry, she would sidle up and ask the lad if he was looking for a room – a somewhat superfluous question as he would already be poring over the small ads, pencil and paper ready in hand.

The next stage in her routine was all too tempting to the young man of her fancy. She'd explain that she had a spare room and then she'd ask if he would be interested in looking at it. Needless to say, the student, erotic thoughts already running riot at the very idea of this voluptuous female offering to take him home, could not agree fast enough – any caution he may have felt would, by this point, have been eradicated by the tidal wave of testosterone-fuelled fantasies that were rapidly scrambling his brain. Willingly, he'd follow her home, blessing his guardian angel and all the saints in heaven for looking so kindly on him. Little did he know that, although his erotic dreams would at least temporarily be realised, everything has its price – a fact of life he was about to learn the hard way.

Margaret would lead the lad straight into her 'spare' room. There, the sight of an inviting double bed would fuel his fantasies even more. And, when Margaret threw herself on top it and patted the counterpane, he'd just know he had arrived in nirvana. With his hormones working at warp speed, the student would fling himself on top of her, tearing at her clothes and struggling to get out of his trousers. In seconds, he'd have penetrated her, luxuriating in the joy of unexpected sex. Then, almost at the height of his euphoria, the wardrobe door would burst open and out would leap – yes, you've guessed it – none other than the bold Batman or, to be more accurate, Johnny boy in a Batman suit.

'Aha!' he would yell. 'Shag my wife, would you? Well, if that's good enough for her, you'll be good enough for me.' And, with that, he would grab the startled, more likely terrified, youth and force him into submission. As a matter of fact, I read on his indictment something along the lines of '. . . and, that, with booted foot and clenched fist, you did force yourself upon him.'

Eventually, however, one of his victims went to the police and reported the assault. The resulting publicity encouraged at least another two or three other victims to come forward.

John was tried for assault and male rape and received seven years at the High Court for his nefarious activities.

Needless to say, he was landed with the name Batman the moment he set foot inside the jail and the name was to follow him throughout his sentence and even into the outside world when he was eventually released. I have no idea what – if anything – happened to his wife. However, the story does not quite end there.

There's no doubt that prisons are hard places to live in and, by this, I don't mean as a punishment. They are hard because you are thrown in among all sorts of people, the majority of whom are ignorant and bad mannered. Most of them have no social skills and are unable to hold a decent conversation, resorting mainly to baiting one another by making outrageous statements about the most personal of things, usually sexually oriented. Getting under someone's skin is perceived as a skill and these cons like nothing better than forcing a reaction from their latest victim – the greater the reaction, the greater the victory.

The trick is not to let them know that they are getting to you. For instance, out of nowhere someone will single you out and say something like, 'I heard you used to be a rent boy.' The way to put an immediate stop to this is to reply along the lines of, 'Aye, I sold my arse for years. Made a right few quid at it too.' You see, if you join in the stupidity, you've got them stymied. But, if you are foolhardy enough to take umbrage or make a heated retort or denial, you are said to have 'bitten' and, from then on, things will only escalate as they take amusement from your outraged reaction.

You have to develop a hide as thick as a rhinoceros to survive mentally in jail. I handled it by giving back the snappy answer but, unfortunately for Batman, he failed miserably in the repartee department.

Funnily enough, although he was in for a sexual offence and a rather unusual one at that, John Higgins was not ostracised or labelled as a 'beast'. I think this was because the cons, being in the main a macho crowd, felt that any man worth his salt should have at least put up a fight and the fact that not one of John's victims retaliated meant that they deserved all they got.

Actually he was fairly well liked, being highly intelligent and always willing to help guys who had difficulty with writing letters and petitions. But this helpfulness did not stop the general loud-mouthed ignorami (Is that a new word I've coined?) continuously baiting him by chanting out the Batman theme, with a loud 'Da-da, da-da, da-da, da-da . . .' and ending in a screamed 'BATMAN!' whenever and wherever he was spotted.

John just could not handle it and always reacted to the taunt by yelling at them to shut up and leave him alone. His face would go crimson and he would duck his head and rush away to his cell, slamming the door to try and block out the sound as more and more guys joined in the fun and took up the theme tune, all chanting in unison and ending with a perfectly timed yell of 'BATMAN!' reverberating throughout the wing. The entertainment lay in John's reaction and the more he reacted, the more they would lay it on.

Things came to a head one evening in the visiting room when one of the visitors, a well-known practical joker, instructed his eight-year-old daughter to approach John's table and confront him. The girl, no doubt thinking it was great fun, waltzed up to John, put her hands on her hips and began piping out the unmistakeable Batman theme. She was the centre of attention, every eye in the visit room focused on her as she stood before her embarrassed victim, da-da, da-da-ing away in her little girl, high-pitched treble voice. Sure it was good fun but it was terribly cruel and John, utterly distraught, abandoned his visitors and fled the room as her final 'BATMAN!!!' was drowned out by the sound of uncontrollable laughter.

I found him in his cell, tears streaming from his eyes. 'Why don't they stop it?' he pleaded with me. 'I can't go anywhere but they're after me. It's driving me mad. What can I do? Look at me – I'm a nervous wreck.' His hands were clasped on his lap and he looked the picture of dejection. 'Everywhere I go, it's the same thing. How can I get them to stop?'

'Listen, John,' I told him, 'they know it annoys you and they do it deliberately to get a laugh at your reaction. If you didn't react, there would be no fun in it for them and they would stop. But, as long as you are going to entertain them with your response, they'll keep it up – you know that yourself. You've got to try and make out that it doesn't annoy you any more.'

'But I *am* annoyed,' he said. 'I can't stand it. Everywhere I go, they keep getting at me. I can't handle it any more.' He looked really forlorn as he sat on his bed twisting his hands.

'Look, John,' I said, 'there is a way to put a stop to it.'

'What . . . How?' He looked hopefully at me.

'Show them it doesn't bother you. Make a joke out of it and, once they see that you're not bothered, they'll leave you alone and find someone else to annoy.'

'And how am I going to do that?'

'Well, it's pretty drastic, John, but I know it will work if you do what I say.'

'Anything,' he said, 'anything that will make them stop.'

'OK then, John, now here's what you have to do. Get yourself a pair of blue tracksuit bottoms, an appropriate T-shirt and then make yourself a cape and a mask out of a black bin liner.'

He was staring at me as if I was mad.

'Then, once you've got all the bits and pieces together, you dress up as Batman and go out into the hall and dive around the recreation room doing the theme and shouting out 'BATMAN!' They'll all get a good laugh but they'll see that it doesn't bother you any more and, once they realise that, they'll stop shouting out at you. I'm telling you, John, it will work.'

'You really think so?' he asked, looking hopefully at me.

'John, I *know* it will work. Believe me, if they think it isn't going to bother you, they'll leave you alone.'

'I'll have to think about this,' he said but there was a glimmer of hope in his voice. 'Give me a couple of days.'

Two or three days later, I was sitting in my cell when John gave a knock on the door and came in with a bundle of clothing in his arm. 'You know,' he said, 'I think you're right. I'm going to do it.'

'Good,' I told him. 'You do this and I guarantee they won't bother you again.'

'Right,' he said, placing some clothes on my bed. 'But there's something you will need to do for me.'

'Anything, John,' I assured him, 'you just need to ask.'

He started to spread out some of the clothes. 'I'll do it as long as you run around beside me dressed as Robin!'

'Fuck off!!!' I told him in no uncertain terms, as I chucked his Robin outfit out into the corridor. My personal rendition of 'Da-da, da-da, da-da, da-da . . .' followed him as he made his way along the corridor to his cell.

Me? Robin? Aye, right!

Stinky Steve – hmm, another strange name but, obviously, as I keep saying, there had to be a good reason to get labelled with a moniker like that.

I ran into Stinky very early on in my sentence when, one evening, I decided to spend my recreation period watching the TV, which was located on the ground floor, up against the wall in the middle of the hall. It was a good TV set but the trouble was that, in a hall that held about a hundred prisoners, there obviously wasn't enough room for all of us to sit in front of the screen. The authorities, in their wisdom, realised this and had placed a long church-like bench on the first landing where we could still get a half decent, although steeply downward, view of the screen. On one of my first nights in PH, I made my way up to the landing and approached the bench (sounds like a court appearance here). I noticed that there was only one man on the actual bench itself while five or six men sat on the slate flooring on either side of it, elbows on the metal guardrail and legs dangling down from the landing. I wondered why they were sitting on the cold slate in preference to the comparative comfort of a warm wooden seat and presumed that the places on the bench were already spoken for but I asked anyway. 'Anybody sitting here?'

The guy on the bench, whose name I was unaware of at that time, looked up at me and held a hand towards the space beside him. 'No,' he said, 'there's plenty of room.'

Indeed there was and I was puzzling over the reason for this when I settled down beside the seat's lone occupant.

I was immediately aware of something odd going on as one or two of the other guys looked round at me then glanced at one another, in an almost conspiratorial manner. There was definitely something going on but I couldn't put my finger on it. All I knew was that they were looking at me with silly knowing grins on their faces. Anyway, I squeezed by and took my seat alongside the other guy, aware once again of quick, sneaky glances being aimed at me.

Something was very definitely in the air, yes, and quite literally too! And that something was the stink of unbelievably strong body odour. Jesus! My eyes almost started watering at the stench and I was aware of the guys on the landing glancing and nudging one another as if sharing some secret. I stood the pong for about two minutes, trying hard to ignore it and hoping that it would somehow or other pass. But, no, the stench grew stronger until, finally, it drove me from my seat and on to the floor alongside the other leg-dangling convicts. I could feel the restrained mirth of the men as they exchanged knowing nods and edged along the landing to make way for me.

Nothing was said but the mystery of the almost empty bench was solved – the guy was absolutely honking. I mean, I've heard of BO but this was BO with a vengeance. How, I asked myself, could anyone possibly let themselves get into such a state that they smelt so strongly? He actually looked quite neat and tidy and he was clean-shaven and bright-eyed, with a smartly ironed shirt and well-pressed trousers. He did not look like a man who just had to be filthy dirty to emit such a stink. So what could be the reason for the malodorous odour emanating from him? It all became clear when his unfortunate story was relayed to me the following day at work

It appeared that Steve Miller was a bit of an amateur arsonist, helping out the odd struggling shopkeeper with a fortuitous fire in the hope that the rich insurance companies would salvage their ailing businesses for them

– a well-proven escape route from premature bankruptcy. Anyway, this Chinese restaurateur found himself with severe cash-flow problems and the only way he could see out of his problem was to have his business, quite literally, go up in smoke. A friend of this particular Chinese trader who had overcome similar financial difficulties in the past suggested that he turn to the tried-and-tested escape route of fire and recommended Steve as experienced exponent of this particular pyrotechnic pastime.

The customary overtures were made and Steve was contracted to attend to the necessary conflagration. However, the Chinese restaurateur was so much in debt that he did not have enough cash in hand to pay the fee for Steve's fire-raising services. So, having agreed a sum, the venal Chinaman decided to add a personal touch of his own to make sure that his business really did go out in a ball of fire or, as it turned out in this case, with a bang – the same bang which would hopefully not only obliterate his business but also remove the necessity of paying Steve his fire-raising fee. With this fiendish plan in mind, the wily Chinaman informed Steve that he would help things along by placing some tins of paint and other highly inflammable materials to one side of the window so as to assist the flames. This meant that Steve would have to press himself up against the bars of the window to enable him to reach inside and lob his incendiary device on to the prepared combustibles, thus guaranteeing a successful conflagration.

Steve, always keen to please, followed the Chinaman's orders meticulously, going up to the open window and leaning hard against the bars to place his bomb in the most advantageous spot. However the Chinaman, in his efforts to avoid paying Steve, had deliberately – and with malice aforethought – left the gas taps in his shop fully open, thus filling the interior with highly explosive fumes. It followed then that, when the unsuspecting Steve punched a large hole in the glass and reached inside with his already-burning incendiary device, he was promptly blasted halfway across the backyard in a ball of fire that burned the clothes from his body and seared his skin like that of a roasted pig.

When the fire brigade arrived they found the unfortunate, half-cooked Steve lying half dead in the yard and rushed him straight to the burns unit of the Royal Infirmary where it was discovered that, along with his other varied and colourful injuries, the searing flames had sealed his sweat glands.

I am no medical man myself but I suppose the fact that you do not have sweat glands doesn't mean that you no longer perspire – it just means that your body must find another way to rid itself of its sweat. In Steve's case, his sweat was obviously exuded as an invisible vapour and it stunk like a skunk to say the least. I dare say Steve was christened Stinky the moment he entered reception at Peterhead, and it is a fact that, even if by some chance he was cured or doused himself in the most exotic scents, he would still forevermore be known as Stinky.

John Harkins – or **Harky** as he was called before attracting the bizarre appellation of **Flame On** – was a weirdo. Even his job before he came to prison made me stop and think. He'd worked as a mortuary attendant. A person who was happy as Larry mucking about with dead bodies? That makes me wonder. I mean, there must be something strange about any *normal* working man choosing to spend his days with the dead and Harky did nothing to dispel my thoughts on that score. Anyone who can walk into a hospital and use medical scalpels to murder and then dissect his wife, his own child and his wife's brother has to be a madman. Because, as incredible as it might seem, that's what the bold Harky did and that was why he ended up in prison doing a lifer with the judge's recommendation that he never be released.

I have no idea why Harky did what he did but what I *do* know is that he ended up in the same prison wing as me and, to all appearances, seemed an ordinary sort of guy although he did have a permanently shifty look about him – as if he was trying hard to be inconspicuous.

Obviously, because of the nature of his offences, Harky was kept under close supervision, particularly in the early part of his sentence. Considered a suicide risk, he was obliged to put his clothes outside his door at night and was not permitted to possess matches or anything that could be deemed remotely usable as a weapon or for self-harming. This is, of course, a nonsense because anyone can, for instance, smash a window and obtain a huge piece of glass with which to wreak havoc on oneself or any unfortunate who happens to attract their harmful intentions. There are literally dozens of items, ranging from sharpened pieces of plastic to needles or razor blades imbedded in toothbrushes which can be, and very often are, converted into lethal weapons in any prison.

However the authorities like to cultivate the appearance of caring, albeit at times a cosmetic one – as if, by merely stating that this, that or the next thing is banned, they can actually prevent any prisoner getting hold of a potential weapon. Anyway, Harky found himself in this situation and as a result he was barred from, among other things, having matches in his possession when he was behind his door.

So, there was Harky one night, behind his door without a match and apparently desperate for a smoke. Now most of the night staff in prison are older guys, long-serving officers nearing retirement, whose only desire is a quiet, uneventful life until pension-drawing time thankfully arrives. Such a person was the screw who was on night patrol when Harky banged on his door and asked for a match to light up his fag. On being told that he was not allowed matches, Harky tried pleading with the screw, saying how desperate he was for a smoke. However, the night patrol maintained his refusal and returned to his desk for a quiet snooze. Refusing to accept the screw's decision, Harky began pounding on his door, the noise reverberating round the wing and rousing the other cons from their innocent slumbers. Needless to say, a chorus of outraged voices rose up against this unseemly disturbance as irate cons demanded silence, forcing the old screw to return to Harky's door to warn him of the possible consequences of his rowdiness, both from official quarters and, more likely, from any number of angry inmates. Unperturbed by such threats, Harky informed the elderly official that he would be happy to cease his banging upon receipt of a match to ignite his nightcap smoke. Against his better judgement, but anxious to appease the disturbed prisoners and re-establish the peace and quiet of the night, the old screw was finally coerced into passing a match under the door to the seemingly desperate Harky.

Once the proud possessor of the match, however, Harky promptly doused himself in liquid wax floor polish and set himself alight. Believe me, the yelling and shouting from the cons faded into total insignificance against the sound of the high-pitched, ululating screams now emanating from Harky's cell. The horrendous screaming must have gone on for two or three minutes and the noise was emphasised by a fascinated silence as the cons listened to the sound of Harky's incineration and the frustrated shouts of the old screw as he fumbled to break the seal on the envelope containing the emergency key.

We all thought Harky was dead but, somehow or other, he survived his attempt at self-immolation and, after months in hospital, he was finally returned to the general population to be promptly christened with the appropriate appellation – Flame On.

The results of his attempt at a fiery suicide were clear to see. His face and entire upper body were pockmarked and scarred where the flesh had melted like a wax candle. Shiny scar tissue drew the skin of his neck tight and pulled his head down on to his chest. It took many operations and years of plastic surgery before he could stand erect again with a face that was just about presentable.

Flame On, for that was now his prison name, could have been forgiven for turning into some sort of recluse. But no! Indeed, the opposite was the case. Flame On revelled in his notoriety and his new nickname, mixing happily with the other cons and even taking to the stage to entertain us with his clarinet playing. In fact, he even developed a macabre sense of humour regarding his condition.

I can clearly recall Flame On coming into one of the cells in Peterhead one evening where three or four of us cons were socialising over a cup of tea. As he walked through the door he looked at one of the guys who was reclining on the bed and addressed him thusly, 'Aye, **Whale**, [the man's huge, blubbery girth made this nickname self-explanatory] you're a right ugly bastard, you know.' This is an example of an incident, as I mentioned elsewhere in this book, where you require the rhinoceros-type skin if you are to avoid a confrontation.

'Oh, aye,' The Whale, a seasoned lifer himself, acknowledged Flame On's observation quite amiably. 'But you're a lot uglier than me.'

'Maybe so,' Flame On retaliated, because getting the last barb in is important in these verbal exchanges if you are to be recognised as a wit. 'But look at you – at least I'm not a fucking *fat* ugly bastard.'

'I know I'm fat,' The Whale responded once again, 'but you're definitely one of the ugliest guys in the jail. Look at the fucking state of you – you've got skin like a crocodile.'

'Oh, aye,' Flame On came back again, 'maybe I have got skin like a crocodile but I've got a good reason for that – I was on fire for five minutes. What's your excuse?'

The Whale gave up at that and went back to reading his paper. It was just another moment of jail black humour repartee.

There must surely be a story attached to anyone with a name like **Rent A Rope** and, as I have stated earlier, cons seem to have a great aptitude for finding a nickname that just seems to fit like a glove. But Rent A Rope? I must admit that it is a little difficult to conjure up a picture of anyone from this title alone. You know, for the life of me, I cannot remember Rent A Rope's real name but I can certainly remember the actions he undertook that resulted in him acquiring such an unusual nom de guerre.

An alcoholic, Rent a Rope shared a flat with a drinking companion in a tenement block somewhere in the Highland town (now, of course, a city) of Inverness. He and his flatmate, another alcoholic, were well-known drunks in the town and they would often be seen together making their rounds of the lower drinking dives in Inverness. Their days usually ended in an alcohol-induced squabble and they often fell foul of the local constabulary with their loud, drunken behaviour.

One night, however, their interminable squabbling developed into something far more sinister and one can only surmise about what was said or done that led to one of these two alkies earning the nickname Rent A Rope. In fact, even poor old Rent A Rope himself had no recollection of the actual events that led to the demise of his flatmate. All he remembers is waking up in the morning and finding his roommate sitting upright in an armchair, dead as the proverbial doornail.

What to do? Rent A Rope found himself in a quandary. Call the police? He ruled that out immediately, feeling that the police would automatically assume he was responsible for the death of his friend. One can only imagine the state of his mind as he cogitated on his problem. There were no marks or bruises on the corpse that he could see, which was good from his point of view. But how could an apparently unmarked body end up dead?

Then he had an idea – he would make it look as if his flatmate had committed suicide. But how could he do that? What method of suicide would seem the most believable or probable? Hmm, that was a hard one. He looked at the body and came to a decision – hang him. Yes, he convinced himself – hang him and it will look like a drunken suicide. It happened all the time, didn't it? And all you needed was a rope. Having made his decision, Rent A Rope now swung into action. All he had to do was string his pal up, call 999 and his problem would be solved – a suicide.

The only problem was that he didn't own a rope. Taking matters by the scruff of the neck, Rent A Rope went to a neighbour's door and enquired if by any chance he could borrow their washing line. No doubt under the impression that our man intended to hang out some laundry, the neighbour produced a suitable length of rope and duly handed it over.

Back in the flat, Rent A Rope found an appropriate fixing for the rope by way of an old-fashioned pulley ring that was still screwed into the ceiling. Soon he was hauling his old drinking pal by the neck, having secured the other end of the rope by tying it on to the cold-water tap in the kitchen. Job done, he stood back to admire his handiwork. Yes, the feet were well off the ground, the rope was taking the strain and everything was looking good, except that was for one thing – he had not considered the effects of rigor mortis on the corpse of his late lamented pal and there he was dangling, knees and arms still bent, in the sitting position he had occupied on the chair.

Rent A Rope tried his best to straighten the stiffened limbs but they just would not unbend for him. Now what to do? The answer seemed simple to him – if the limbs wouldn't straighten themselves out, he would have to help them. Working with a will, he brought in an old baseball bat that was kept in the hallway, in case of unwelcome visitors, and set about the corpse with heavy swings of the bat. This should straighten out the legs and arms no bother, he told himself and indeed it did. Satisfied that the body was nicely draped on the end of the washing line, Rent A Rope then made his 999 call and reported the unfortunate suicide of his flatmate.

Needless to say, the autopsy soon disclosed the broken bones and this information was immediately relayed to the local constabulary, resulting in the apprehension of the bold

Rent A Rope. With no explanation and the neighbour's evidence that he had lent the rope to you-know-who, the outcome of the trial was a foregone conclusion. Lucky to be found guilty of just manslaughter, he was sentenced to ten years' imprisonment and ended up in Peterhead, where he was promptly christened and known forever after as Rent A Rope.

I know I said that I was not going to go into the harder side of prison life but **Rab The Cat**'s story certainly has a humorous slant to it and I feel that I am justified in including it in my modest anthology of prison characters. The incident that led to Robert Meechan being dubbed Rab The Cat occurred many years before I ever arrived in Peterhead but it has gone down in prison folklore and it offers some insight into the tough sort of characters who were sent there.

In prison, whenever there is any reference made to a 'cat', you immediately think of two things – a 'cat burglar' and the 'cat-o'-nine-tails'. In this case, it's the latter definition that's relevant. Rab The Cat goes down in penal history as the last man to be to be lashed – or 'given the cat' – in Peterhead Prison.

The circumstances were these. Robert Meechan was in the punishment block for assaulting a prison officer when he made a special request to be allowed to attend Sunday Bible class. It is a fact that Scottish prison governors have always been very keen on getting those in the cells to attend church and Bible classes. The bold Robert's request to attend any religious meeting, therefore, both impressed and pleased the governor and permission was readily granted. But Robert had a more devious reason for attending Bible class than seeking reformation by listening to the preaching of the Word.

The tobacco-barren punishment block had him at the end of his tether and, frantic for a smoke, Robert decided desperate measures were called for. He knew that the church organist smoked a pipe and, therefore, it followed that he would have a tobacco pouch somewhere on his person.

The Bible class was going strong, its large attendance due more to breaking the tedium of prison than any desire to be nearer to God. The organist was in full tilt, belting out 'Onward Christian Soldiers' or something like it, when Robert rose to his feet and went forward to embrace him. However, under cover of the 'embrace' Robert was actually doing a quick check of the petrified organist's pockets, searching for the elusive tobacco pouch. He succeeded in his mission and was clutching the tobacco pouch when he was tackled by the supervising screws and thrown to the floor. Throughout the struggle Robert held the pouch so tightly that it was impossible for the screws to get it from him. Finally, a compromise was made and Robert was told that, if he gave back the pouch, he could keep the tobacco. This was agreed and a victorious Robert was left with his desired smoke and the organist got his pouch back, with the governor compensating him for the stolen tobacco. However, the terrified soldier of Christ never returned to the prison again.

For the Bible class escapade, Robert was sentenced to twenty lashes of the cat-o'-nine-tails, which were delivered with him stretched on a triangular frame in the prison bath house. (The brass mountings for the frame can still be seen there to this day.) When he was untied from the frame, the bold Robert performed a backflip, landed on his feet and declared, 'Give me a couple more fags and I'll take the same again.'

He must have really meant it too because, three years later, in Parkhurst Prison, he assaulted a prison officer and was once again sentenced to 'the cat'.

I actually met Arthur **The Godfather** Thomson myself on two occasions in 1967. The first time was in the Raven Club, a drinking den in a lane close to Queen Street Station in the centre of Glasgow. The second time was a few days later in Arthur's flat in a rundown tenement building at 5 Sword Street, Dennistoun, when we met to conclude the business that had been discussed in the club. Up until then, I had only known Arthur by reputation but he was easy enough to get on with and we concluded our business to our mutual satisfaction and profit. The only time I ever saw him after that was when he was visiting his son – also named Arthur but better known as **Fatboy** – in Glenochil Prison, near Stirling.

I don't know exactly when Arthur Thomson was jailed but I do know that, sometime in the late fifties, he was sentenced to four years' imprisonment on a charge of reset, i.e. knowingly receiving stolen property. I find it odd that, although many thousands of words have been written about Arthur and his rise through the ranks of underworld Glasgow, there is very little, if anything, known about how he handled his time in jail.

Having been sentenced at Glasgow's High Court meant, of course, that Arthur served the first few weeks of his sentence in the Bar-L, as Glasgow's grim Barlinnie Prison is known, before being shipped off to Peterhead to serve out his time. From everything I've heard, Arthur settled down quickly, not making any waves or throwing his weight around, simply getting on with his time with as little bother as possible. The added advantage of having a reputation as a hard man and street fighter meant he was left well alone by the bully boys and Arthur soon settled into prison life.

However, while he was in Barlinnie Prison awaiting transfer to PH, an unsuspected facet of Arthur's character came to light – it seems that he enjoyed playing practical jokes. While you were in the Bar-L waiting for the dreaded draft bus, you were always put to work in the mailbag shop. Believe me, the mailbag shop was a drab, sense-dulling place at the best of times, and with rows of bored men sitting on long benches sewing heavy canvas, eight stitches to the inch, day in, day out, any diversion was always welcome.

About once a week, and with the connivance of the screws, who were every bit as bored as their criminal charges, Arthur would dress like a doctor in an officer's white coverall and, holding a clipboard, he would call out a guy's name and number. Arthur would then get the victim, always a first offender, to strip off in the storeroom for a 'medical inspection' before running off with his clothes. It helped to lighten the day and gave everyone a laugh as the guy went scuttling about, swathed in mailbag canvas, searching for his kit.

With limited resources though, most of the pranks were pretty childish. Sending a 'rookie' to the PO's desk for a two-headed needle, sewing up the sleeves of someone's jacket, spreading black wax or strategically placing a needle on some guy's seat – these were examples of the usual run of things. All these ploys were good for a giggle and broke up the grinding monotony of the day, giving the cons something to smile about for a change.

However, the sewing needle placed on someone's chair was not the sort of stuff Arthur liked – he was more subtle than that. For instance, an older guy working alongside him in the mailbag party had a bad leg and used a walking stick to help himself get around. Once or twice a week, Arthur would get hold of the old guy's walking stick, remove its rubber tip and saw a little bit off the end before replacing the tip again. Everyone else was in on the game and the old guy never noticed the gradual shortening of his walking stick. After a couple weeks, the noticeably hunched-over old guy was demanding medical treatment for his 'bad back'. Arthur ran that particular joke for about three weeks until, on the day before his transfer to PH, he presented the suffering man with a new, full-length walking stick and effected an immediate 'miraculous' cure.

At that time in Barlinnie, it was common practice to be locked up three to a cell and Arthur was sharing with the oft-mentioned Wullie Leitch when a third man, a country type experiencing his first stay in jail, was allocated to share with them. Being, for want of a better word, sitting tenants, Arthur and Wullie had first choice of the sprung bunk beds, leaving only a wooden, fold-down platform for the latest arrival. Once the new guy was settled in, Wullie was surprised when Arthur started talking about the poltergeist that haunted the cell. The new chap seemed a little nervous at this information but Arthur assured him that he would come to no harm as the ghost only moved things around during the night.

In the course of the evening, Arthur surreptitiously slipped out the hinge pins of the bed and during the night, little by little, pulled the platform away from the wall until the rookie's head was actually under the bottom bunk. Once everything was set up both Arthur and Wullie started lobbing books and mugs about until the young guy suddenly woke up, banging his head off the underside of the bunk and freaking out with fear.

'The ghost! The ghost!' he yelled, shaking and pulling at Arthur who seemed to be in a sound sleep. 'The fucking ghost! It's here. It's been pulling me about. I want out of here!' he shouted and lunged for the alarm bell.

It took both Arthur and Wullie about ten minutes to calm the youth down, only convincing him to go back to bed when Arthur agreed to sleep on the platform himself for the rest of the night. The following morning the lad ran down to the hall desk demanding an immediate cell change but Arthur, knowing that the other cons would now try and take liberties with him, showed his kinder side by explaining about the hinge pins and how he had been the one who had moved the bed. The lad at last saw the joke and Arthur convinced him to remain in the cell where he would be under his protection from the other cons.

In Peterhead, too, Arthur made his mark in more ways than one. Tying a fish to the bedsprings in a victim's cell would have the occupant scrubbing it out for days until the rotten carcase was discovered. Piercing a plastic pisspot was always good for a laugh and snapping the handle off the door lock just before lockup time got both the con and the screws going wild. However, I think Arthur's greatest achievement was when he was working in the old quarry, the main workplace in Peterhead until the early 1950s. One day, he went round with his hammer and chipped the corners off a special order of granite blocks that were awaiting despatch.

In fact, along with his practical joking, Arthur handled his time well. He never gave the screws any trouble (except for the granite blocks incident, that is) and he never allowed himself to become involved in prison violence or politics. He simply 'did his time' and certainly gave no hint that he would one day rise to the top of Glasgow's criminal underworld and become known to one and all as **The Godfather**.

There was this screw – I forget his real name – we called **The RSM**. Standing for Regimental Sergeant Major, it aptly reflected his strict military attitude and his penchant for highly polished boots. He was one of the old school, who insisted on wearing his military medal ribbons on his uniform. You used to get a lot of screws like him in prisons years ago – ex-servicemen, unable to resist the lure of the uniform, who joined the Prison Service when they finished their military careers. Another bulled-up boots merchant, The RSM also sported a bristling, well-trimmed, military-type moustache. He was a stickler for discipline and would tell you off for wearing your shirt outside your trousers or having your hands in your pockets. Mostly, of course, we just ignored him – it was all just an act anyway. However, when The RSM was on duty there was one guy in A Hall who would make a point of marching past him with his arms swinging. Then, one day, The RSM fell into his trap.

'Jackson!' The RSM snapped out one day when the bold Jackson marched past him, bringing the said con to a halt.

'Sir?' Jackson carried on with his charade, snapping sharply to attention in front of him.

The RSM rocked on his heels for a moment or two, assessing the prisoner in front of him. 'Been in the forces, Jackson?' he finally barked out.

'Of course, sir,' Jackson replied, speaking in a fine militaristic style and struggling to conceal his glee that his bait had been taken at last.

'I thought so,' said The RSM, nodding his head approvingly. 'And which corps did you serve with?'

'The Royal Army Service Corps, sir,' said Jackson immediately, showing he was equal to the occasion. Besides, he was actually telling the truth.

'A fine corps, Jackson,' The RSM said in a congratulatory tone. 'A fine corps. And how long did you serve?'

Jackson hesitated a little before delivering his bombshell to The RSM. Then, in a clear clipped voice, he snapped out his devastating reply. 'Six weeks, sir – then I deserted. Do you think I'm fucking stupid?' He then executed a perfect about turn, stamped his foot down and marched away, arms swinging shoulder-high in parody of militarism.

The RSM was almost apoplectic, his face going beetroot red as he gasped for breath in an effort to formulate an adequate reply to this heresy. 'Scum! Scum!' he yelled, finally getting some words out. 'I should have known better.' His voice rang round the landing but it was almost drowned out by the laughter of those cons who had been close enough to witness the event.

'Aye, so you should have, you fucking halfwit!' the unrepentant Jackson fired back at him, as he right-wheeled to enter his cell, a pleased smile pasted on his face.

There is a game played in the jail that sometimes runs for weeks as the joker prepares the ground to make his target 'bite', as they say. Ronnie Williamson, known also as **Ron The Con** of course, once spent several weeks chatting away with one of the guys, all the time picking up bits of relevant information that he would piece together, ready to utilise them when the time was ripe. It was after just such a fact-gathering exercise that, one day in the workshop, Ron The Con happened to mention that he once had a girlfriend in Clydebank.

One of the prisoners in the group, Dominic something or other, named **Dom The Dome** by virtue of his completely bad pate, raised his head at this piece of information and ventured a question.

'Whereabouts in Clydebank did your girlfriend live?' he asked.

'Erm . . .' Ron appeared to give the question some thought. 'I forget the name of the street,' he finally admitted, 'but I remember that the police station was on it.'

'Manor Street,' The Dome informed him. 'I was born there.' Then, obviously interested, he went on to question Ron further. 'Do you remember the address, the street number I mean?'

'Nah,' Ron shook his head. 'It was a long time ago.' He appeared to think for a moment then he said, 'I don't remember the number but it was the second close in the block going away from the cop shop.'

'Fuck me!' The Dome exclaimed, looking really surprised. 'I was born up that close. What was your girlfriend's name? I'll probably know her.'

By this time we were all tuned in, one or two of us remarking on how coincidental it all was.

'Oh, it was years ago now,' said Ron, obviously struggling to remember. 'Wait a minute – it's coming back to me.' He stretched his thinking silence out as we all waited for his answer. Finally he nodded his head. 'Aye,' he said, 'I remember now. It was Margaret – Margaret Wilson.'

'What!' The Dome looked at him in surprise. 'Margaret Wilson?' he said. 'That was my mother's maiden name.'

Ron The Con looked at him, an astonished expression on his face. Then he leapt to his feet, arms outstretched.

'Son!' he loudly exclaimed, stepping forward to hug The Dome. 'My long-lost son!'

There was silence for a second or two and then, as we realised what Ron had been up to, we folded up with laughter.

Dom The Dome, although red-faced, accepted it well. He had taken the bait like a big Tay salmon and been well and truly hooked. It was a story that would go down well that night during recreation.

30
THE END OF THE ROAD

It is strange but also a fact that you tend to remember the funnier side of prison life once you leave the place. Maybe it is an unconscious mental defence against the anguish and hard times we all went through but it is true and, if you speak to ex-cons most of them will say things like 'It wasn't that bad' or 'We had plenty of good laughs' and they will relate a string of amusing tales similar to the ones I have told you in this book. But ask them about the hard times and you will find a hesitancy – an almost unconscious inability to recall the bad times inside. It is as if they have suffered selective memory loss – as if there's a subliminal need to suppress the bad memories. And even when they do recall some incident that hurt them, they will turn it into a joke.

The names I have mentioned throughout this book were just some of the characters I 'done time' with in Peterhead. And there were others. People like **Karate Joe**, a little fat screw that would walk around the landing doing his best to look dangerous. He actually reminded me of Peter Sellers in his cinematic role as Clouseau, the bumbling French detective, in the way he would suddenly spin round, hands raised, ready to karate chop an imagined attacker. This was his way of letting us know that he was a dangerous adversary should anyone be thinking of attacking him. He also had the habit of suddenly chopping at the guard rail with the edge of his hand as he patrolled along the landing. Right enough, he did give us all a good laugh one night when he chopped the rail so hard that his wristwatch flew off and shattered into pieces on the bottom flat.

Then there was **Tulip**, another screw, so named because of his big pouty lips and his tendency to blush like a teenager whenever anyone chirped at him. **Princess Anne** was another one, his remarkably equine-looking head immediately attracting that nickname.

And they all knew their nicknames too. There was one time when Princess Anne shouted from the yard up to a prisoner's window.

'Who is it?' The con shouted back from a recumbent position on his bed.

'It's me,' Princess Anne came back at him. 'Come to your window.' He was probably going to tell the guy to take in some socks that were draped over the outside bars to dry.

'Who's me?' The voice from the cell rose again.

There was a few moments' silence and then we heard a lower, slightly hushed voice replying, 'It's Princess Anne.' He was a screw who knew his place all right.

Then there was **Yogi Bear**, always easy-going, jovial and fair. And there's a **Bootsie** in nearly every jail in the country – ex-military types who insist on bulling the toes of their enormous boots until they shine like glass. **The Screaming Skull**'s physiognomy leaves you in no doubt as to the origin of his nickname.

Of course, at the end of it all, an important question must be asked – does prison work? The short answer is no. And the longer you keep people in prison, the less likely it is to work. The reason for that is quite simple – after so many years, you get used to life in jail and jail becomes your life. It holds no fears because you have slipped into a way of life that has become normal for you. There are even several life-sentence prisoners in Scotland today who have point blank refused to pick up their beds and go. Others continue to delay their release by telling the governor and the parole board that they intend to re-offend if they get out. And, if they still get out despite doing this, they are not overly concerned about going back. It is a fact that ex-cons experience more problems when they leave jail than they ever had to cope with inside. That is the reason jail does not work for the really long-term prisoner.

One guy who put Peterhead into perspective was the ubiquitous Walter Ellis. Watty served a full fourteen years out of a twenty-one year sentence for armed robbery and, barely three months after his release, he was back in the High Court again on a similar charge. Found guilty, he was asked by the judge if he had anything to say in mitigation before sentence was handed down.

Watty had, indeed, plenty to say. He told the judge that he had been released after fourteen years in Peterhead Prison without so much as one day's preparation for the outside world. He said that he had never received any trade training and, in all that time, he hadn't seen a tree or a dog or a child. The whole world had moved on – even the district where he lived had been rebuilt – and, when he'd asked the governor to supply him with a map, his request was denied. He was released after fourteen years with just a travel warrant and one week's social security money with which to begin a new life. Once on the outside, he had felt totally disorientated and completely out of touch. Decimal currency had been introduced while he'd been inside and it was a complete mystery to him. The increased traffic was a total hazard – once, Watty claimed, he had run after a corporation bus and tried to jump on board but bounced off the back because they had moved the doors to the front. In an alien world, unemployed and unemployable, he had simply drifted back into crime and now found himself before the court again.

The judge was rather sceptical about these allegations and told Watty that he had intended handing down a severe sentence. However, having listened to him speak, he decided to defer sentence until he had looked into the matter. On Watty's return to court a few days later, the judge told him that he had been shocked to discover that everything he had said was true. After announcing his disapproval of the Prison Service and deploring its total lack of any pre-release training for Watty, the judge, almost apologetically, sentenced him to a minimum term of three years.

I was out on the exercise yard the day Watty returned from court. Everyone had tipped him for a twelve – a ten at the very least – but there he was smiling all over his face and shouting out the window at me, 'Got a three, Bing,' he yelled. 'I'll be out before you!' And, in fact, he was. But I had the last laugh because, unfortunately, Watty later copped a twelve-year sentence and I was actually out before him.

I was finally released from prison in 1987 – twelve years and six months since I was sent down. My goodbyes in Peterhead were few and casual at that. I had always taken care not to establish any enduring friendships and the three or four long-termers I had mostly associated with were equally offhand. We exchanged addresses and phone numbers – maybe we would get in touch or run into one another again, maybe not. It was all low-key and anticlimactic.

There was just one last hurdle to clear and that was a return trip on the prison bus to either Barlinnie or Saughton Prison for final release. A few years previously, the governor would simply have issued rail warrants and bussed the men into Aberdeen to catch the train home. However, even in the short space of time they had to wait for the train, the newly released prisoners created so much mayhem in Aberdeen that the police barred them from the city, insisting that they be bussed south and released from their local prisons.

Peterhead certainly held a lot of memories for me, both good and bad, and I was glad to be leaving but I couldn't help looking back at the place as the bus drove off. I remember craning my neck to catch a last glimpse of the workshop chimney – my first sight of the jail and now, hopefully, my last. When the chimney stack finally disappeared behind the shoulder of a hill for the last time, I thought, almost aloud, Well, that's that! But I continued to stare in its direction for another few seconds as if to make sure it really had gone. With the last sight of the prison, the air in the bus seemed to lighten and I felt relief, a relaxation of the tension that had so insidiously become part of my daily life. There were half a dozen other guys on the bus that day and I'm sure every one of them felt the same sense of release. Then someone cracked a joke and we laughed together as the pressure of Peterhead fell away.

But I did have one last reminder of the sort of people I had left behind – five of my companions on that bus had visibly scarred faces and, out of a total of seven men, two of them were minus an eye. What are the odds on that being the case with seven ordinary men picked at random?

I remember thinking about that as I turned round and faced the front of the bus, looking at the road ahead and wondering what was coming next.

EPILOGUE
DID IT WORK?

So there we have it. Peterhead – hundreds of misfits lumped together and expected to become rehabilitated but the place just did not work. The cons have a saying up there – 'If you come to Peterhead once, you will always come back for more.' It happened to me – eighteen months in 1967 and a massive twenty years in 1974 so obviously no rehab for me.

And after the twenty? Well, believe me, that didn't work either. But, then again, that's another story . . .